S0-AZH-983

SPEAKING OF GOD TODAY

SPEAKING OF GOD TODAY

Jews and Lutherans in Conversation

edited by PAUL D. OPSAHL
MARC H. TANENBAUM

FORTRESS PRESS Philadelphia

The essay "The People and the Land," by Zwi Werblowski, has appeared in substantially the same form under the title "Israel: The People and the Land" in *Peoples and Conflict in the Middle East. A Preliminary Report for Study* (Philadelphia: Office of the General Assembly of the United Presbyterian Church in the United States of America, 1973), pp. 107–112.

Biblical quotations from the Revised Standard Version of the Bible, copyrighted 1946 and 1952 by the Division of Christian Education of the National Council of the Churches of Christ in the United States of America, are used by permission.

Library of Congress Catalog Card Number 73-89083

ISBN 0-8006-0275-7

4066K73 Printed in U.S.A. 1-275

Contents

Editors' Introduction

Why Jewish-Lutheran theological conversations? The answer to such a question is embedded in the theological and historical interaction of Jews and Lutherans, including the perceptions and misperceptions that many Jews and Lutherans have held about each other and about each other's faith claims across the last four and one-half centuries.

From a Jewish perspective, an effort to sort out and evaluate the meaning of its experience in the Western world compels the Jewish community to confront its relationship with Lutheranism, Lutheran people and congregations, and Lutheran theology. It is probably no hyperbole to assert that for the majority of Jews today, Lutheranism continues to be regarded as "quintessential Protestantism," the archetypical non-Roman Christianity. The person of Martin Luther seems to dominate the emergence of the Reformation as much to Jewry as to most Christians.

From a Lutheran perspective, the life of the church in its biblical, theological, liturgical, and pastoral dimensions leads to examination of the issues of Christian identity vis-à-vis Judaism, e.g., the historic Jesus as a Jew, and the grounding of the church in the context of ideas and values of first-century rabbinic Judaism. Moreover, the relationship of the contemporary church with Jews and Judaism is so important for Christian self-understanding, and the improvement of relationships so crucial, that efforts toward clarity and deepened understanding today can only be welcomed.

At the heart of both Jewish and Christian identities lies the promise of God to raise up and preserve for his purposes a unique people. Over the centuries both communities have claimed to be that people—with varying emphases on the exclusivity of that claim. Within each of these religious traditions, there have been distinctive teachings which have shaped the faith and life of each. A consideration of law (Torah), for example, is essential for understanding Judaism. Justification by grace through faith, a distinction between law and gospel, and the so-called doctrine of the "two kingdoms" become pivotal for understanding how faith and life have been shaped within the Lutheran tradition.

Would mutual exploration of faith issues be a way to create beginnings for genuinely constructive relations between these two religious communities, and to make a contribution to the broader Christian-Jewish encounter, especially in the United States? An international consultation on the church and the Jewish people, convened under the auspices of the Lutheran World Federation in Løgumkloster, Denmark, in 1964, strongly encouraged this approach for its member churches as it stated: "It is a Christian responsibility to seek respectfully to understand both the Jewish people and their faith. Therefore responsible conversations between Christians and Jews are to be desired and welcomed. Such conversations presuppose the existence of common ground on which Christians and Jews may meet, as well as points of difference."[1]

In the hope that such theological exchange would be worthwhile, the Division of Theological Studies of the Lutheran Council in the U.S.A.[2] and the Interreligious Affairs Department of the American Jewish Committee[3] convened an academic colloquium in the spring of 1969. The modest purpose of this initial conversation was to explore the possibilities for further fruitful theological talks between Lutherans and Jews. To achieve this, attention was focused on two themes central to each tradition: law and grace; election and the people of God. The four papers presented comprise Part One of the present volume. As is true of all essays in this book, they did not represent consensus attained, either between the two religious traditions or within the Lutheran or Jewish groups. They were prepared as contributions for study and discussion, and as such do not necessarily reflect the point of view of the group or of the sponsoring organizations. Without exception, however, these papers did expose areas where fruitful inquiry and discussion could be profitably pursued.

This colloquium, the first such national-level conversation involving scholars from the major bodies of American Lutheranism and all branches —Conservative, Orthodox, and Reform—of Judaism, was considered to

1. See the Appendix, "The Church and the Jewish People," p. 166. This document's condemnation of anti-Semitism and encouragement to root out its traces in religious education curricula, represent one of the earliest postwar declarations on these sensitive issues from within a world confessional family.

2. The Lutheran Council in the U.S.A. is an agency for cooperative study and service whose participating church bodies are The American Lutheran Church, the Lutheran Church in America, and The Lutheran Church—Missouri Synod. The combined membership of these three churches is approximately 95 percent of the total Lutheran constituency in the United States.

3. The American Jewish Committee was founded in 1906 to protect the civil and religious rights of Jews throughout the world and to promote improved intergroup and interreligious relationships.

have been an exceptionally promising initial probe. In addition to the significant theological issues which were presented and discussed, one of the richest aspects of the consultation was the frank and mutually respectful conversation which took place in response to the papers.[4]

It became clear at the first conversation that there were a number of crucial items for the interreligious agenda which should be covered with much more thoroughness and in some kind of logical progression.[5] The significance of "the land," for example, and the transforming force of the Holocaust had surfaced early as particularly pressing problems. The question of the Lutheran "two kingdoms" ethic[6] together with its application (or misapplication), and the ambivalent attitudes of Martin Luther toward the Jews[7] were problems acutely felt by the partners in conversation. In subsequent colloquia, as Part Two of this book reflects, participants examined together the issues of promise, land, people, and state in the light of biblical interpretation and historical theology, as well as current concerns. It was the view of many of the discussants that while the two heritages might view things differently at several points, the modern state of Israel and Middle Eastern relations ought to be viewed particularly in terms of justice, if not necessarily theology, and that all men of good will should unite in pressing for the settlement of critical problems with maximum feasible justice and the least injustice for all.[8]

The essays in Part Three speak directly to a fundamental theological question confronting both Judaism and Christianity: How do we speak of God today? In every age Jews and Christians have sought to articulate and communicate their understanding of God's revelation in light of the salient factors which shape and condition their respective communities' theology and life. Among the forces now affecting both synagogue and

4. For a report on the initial colloquium, held in New York City, see *Lutheran Quarterly* 21, no. 4 (November 1969): 401–59, 501.

5. Reports from the second and third colloquia were drawn up by John Reumann for the *Journal of Ecumenical Studies.* Material on the spring, 1970, meeting at Concordia Seminary, St. Louis, appears in *JES* 8, no. 2 (Spring 1971): 497–99. The third colloquium at Brandeis University, Waltham, Massachusetts, held in November, 1971, is covered in *JES* 9, no. 2 (Spring 1972): 448–50. The fourth and most recent consultation took place at the Evangelical Lutheran Theological Seminary, Columbus, Ohio, in the spring of 1973.

6. Perhaps more properly considered as the two ways God works among mankind: in the church through gospel and grace; in the world through reason and justice.

7. This is dealt with by Uriel Tal in his essay in this volume, but cf. also Franklin Sherman's introduction to the essay, "On the Jews and Their Lies," in *Luther's Works,* vol. 47, *The Christian in Society IV* (Philadelphia: Fortress Press, 1971), pp. 123–36; also Aarne Siirala, "Luther and the Jews," in *Lutheran World* 11, no. 3 (July 1964): 337–57.

8. Cf. Reumann in *JES* (Spring 1971), p. 448.

church are the societal, cultural, and theological pluralisms, and—for all Jewish-Christian encounter in particular—the haunting specter of the Nazi Holocaust.

To address spiritual and human issues theologically as responsible members of a religious community is an inescapable task of both Christian and Jew today. Have we learned to cope with evil and its brutalizing consequences? What theological and moral resources are available for making some meaningful contribution toward sensitizing consciences and the will of the human family to prevent the repetition of any holocaust against any people? On the level of common humanity, therefore, Christians and Jews should make common cause to the fullest extent in matters of civil and social concerns. On the level of religious commitment, mutual sharing of faith becomes one way for separate religious communities to begin to consider pluralism more as a resource than as simply a problem.[9]

At the time that plans were being made for the first of the four colloquia whose papers appear in this volume, a request came to the Division of Theological Studies of the Lutheran Council to study the relationships of Christians and Jews in the interest of finding a common Lutheran position. The Division decided that for this particular assignment it would develop its stance from within a living, theological-personal exchange such as could be cultivated in the colloquia, and that from within this dialogical context it would attempt to work out biblical and confessional principles applicable for Lutheran Christians. It is out of such an experience, in which suspicions and misunderstandings could be

9. "Dialogue" on matters of faith, and questions of "mission" and "witness" have long been sensitive areas both in Christian and in Jewish circles, and the understandings and approaches have varied. A consultation on "The Church and the Jewish People," convened in April, 1973, under the auspices of the Lutheran World Federation in Neuendettelsau, Germany, addressed Lutherans in the following way on these issues:

"On the level of religious commitment, Christians should invite Jews to engage in a mutual sharing of faith. Christians are not in a position to tell their Jewish neighbors that they should engage in such activities nor can they prescribe the manner in which this should be done. But Christian faith is marked by the impulse to bear witness to the grace of God in Jesus Christ. To bear such witness is intended as a positive, not a negative act. Witness, whether it be called 'mission' or 'dialogue,' includes a desire both to know and to be known more fully. When we speak of a mutual sharing of faith we do not endorse syncretism. But we understand that when Christians and Jews speak to each other about matters of faith, there will be an exchange which calls for openness, honesty, love, and mutual respect. One cannot reveal his faith to another without recognizing the real differences that exist and being willing to take the risk of confronting these differences. We are using the words 'witness' and 'mission' and 'dialogue,' which have come to be labels for distinctive ways of sharing faith. These words have a different content for different Christians. We see problems in the use of these words and urge that Christian people give attention to exploring their meanings."

cleared up, and where Christians (and Jews) could reexamine their theologies in light of the other's faith and claims, that the appended "Guidelines" should be understood. When trust and confidence are established, it becomes possible to share openly "assumptions, prejudices, traditions, and convictions."[10] Within this same setting, too, credibility is lent to the assertion: "There is no biblical or theological basis for anti-Semitism. Supposed theological or biblical bases for anti-Semitism are to be examined and repudiated. Conscious or unconscious manifestations of discrimination are to be opposed."[11]

To speak of Jewish-Christian dialogue in any serious way today means that Christians and Jews have no alternative but to try to come to terms with a beclouded theological and historical past. Both must try to grapple with the true and ultimate religious—and human—questions of theodicy, God's hiddenness, God's promises, God's faithfulness, human arrogance and perversity, dehumanization, acceptance of personal responsibility, and, most difficult of all, contrition, repentance, and forgiveness. It is hoped that this volume will contribute to the process of clarifying and sorting out those issues which desperately need attention, and that it will be of constructive usefulness to our constituencies as well as of service to the building of that larger community of mankind which also is of God.

We are indebted to our staff colleagues, William G. Rusch of the Lutheran Council in the U.S.A. and A. James Rudin and Gerald Strober of the American Jewish Committee, for their assistance both in coordinating the colloquia and in preparing the volume for publication.

Paul D. Opsahl
Executive Secretary
Division of Theological Studies
Lutheran Council in the U.S.A.

Marc H. Tanenbaum
National Director
Interreligious Affairs
The American Jewish Committee

10. See "Some Observations and Guidelines," p. 164.
11. See "Some Observations and Guidelines," p. 165.

Contributors

Michael Wyschogrod
—Professor of Philosophy, Baruch College of the City University of New York

Horace D. Hummel
—Professor of Old Testament, Valparaiso University

Nils A. Dahl
—Professor of New Testament, The Divinity School, Yale University

Seymour Siegel
—Professor of Theology, Jewish Theological Seminary of America

Ronald M. Hals
—Professor of Old Testament, Evangelical Lutheran Theological Seminary, Columbus, Ohio

Zwi Werblowsky
—Professor of Comparative Religion, Hebrew University, Jerusalem

Theodore G. Tappert
—until his death Professor at Lutheran Theological Seminary at Philadelphia

Uriel Tal
—Professor of Modern Jewish History, Tel Aviv University

George W. Forell
—Professor of Religion, School of Religion, University of Iowa

Lionel Rubinoff
—Professor of Social Science and Philosophy, Trent University, Peterbourough, Ontario

Franklin Sherman
—Professor of Christian Ethics, Lutheran School of Theology at Chicago

PART ONE

LAW—GRACE—ELECTION

1.

The Law: Jews and Gentiles

MICHAEL WYSCHOGROD

Several years ago, there appeared a Hebrew book that aroused some interest in rabbinic circles in Europe, Israel, and the United States and very little interest anywhere else. It was a collection of responsa[1] from the years 1939–45, the period that saw the destruction of most of European Jewry. The rabbinic responsum is, of course, a well-established and respected form of rabbinic literature; in it, a given rabbi responds in writing to a *she-elah,* a problem arising in some area of life the answer to which is given by the rabbi from his knowledge of the Torah. These questions can deal with just about any area of life, from differences in the interpretation of a business contract to difficulties over the permissibility of certain foods in the light of the new food technology. But these responses were different. They came from the victims of the ghettos and death camps of the new order, and the problems they raised were very urgent and not very usual. A mother of several children had been ordered by the camp commandant to choose one of them for the gas chamber, otherwise all would be taken. Should she refrain from making the selection and let all of them perish or should she select one and, if so, which one? Was it necessary to fast on Yom Kippur in the death camps or did the danger to life suspend the commandment? Was it permissible to take on non-Jewish identity if there was no other way to escape deportation and almost certain death, or was this step a transgression which must be avoided at all costs, even death? Such questions and many others are answered in the responsa, calmly and always replete with relevant citations from the Bible, Talmud, and post-talmudic literature—as relevant as any citation can be under such circumstances. Sometimes the responsa are lenient, permitting what would not normally be permitted. But sometimes they refuse to yield, insisting on obedience even

1. Ephroim Oshri, *Sheeloth Utshovoth Mimaamakim,* 2 vols. (New York: privately published, 1959, 1963).

in the light of the most dire consequences. This was Jewish life during World War II.

In his *Search for a Method*[2] the French existentialist philosopher Jean-Paul Sartre recounts his first contact with Marxism. He tells us that he was very unimpressed by Marxist dialectics since he had just emerged from immersion in the system of Hegel, a thought system richer and more profound than that of Marx. But he could not get away from the incarnation of Marxism: the French working class. Here was an inarticulate mass that lived and breathed its Marxism and this he could not dismiss. So it is with the problem of law and grace, or law and gospel as this issue agitates Paul, Marcion, Luther, and so many others in the long history of the discussion between Judaism and Christianity. Were it not for the fact that in Paul's time there were Jews who obeyed the law (or the Torah, as we shall soon see), the issue would have been an exercise in the history of ideas and would have lacked the immediacy it has in his writings. And only because there are Jews today who still obey (or try to obey) the law, the matter is still outstanding. There are Jews today who refrain from lighting fires on the Sabbath (Exod. 35:3), put on their phylacteries in the morning (Exod. 3:19), abstain from sexual intercourse with their wives during the period of menstruation and for seven days thereafter (Lev. 15:19–24), and do not wear garments made of wool and flax (Deut. 22:11). Admittedly, the matter is complicated by the fact that the Jews who do all these things are a minority of all Jews in the world. Many Jews have simply stopped obeying various portions of the Torah without having given the matter much thought one way or the other. Reform, and to some extent Conservative, Jews have given the matter thought and concluded that certain portions of the law are not relevant today and need not be obeyed. But it is with Orthodox Jews that Paul was concerned and it is with Orthodox Judaism that the issue has been joined over the course of the centuries. If I then proceed from an Orthodox perspective it is because it is my perspective, and the one from which this problem is most alive.

First of all, I would like to confess that it is difficult for me to see how a thinking Orthodox Jew can avoid coping with the Paul-Luther criticism of the law. For me, it has been the only criticism that I have found really interesting. Sometimes I have almost found myself believing that only an observant Jew, a Jew who tries to live up to the commandments

2. Jean-Paul Sartre, *Search for a Method* (New York: Knopf, 1963).

of the Torah, can truly understand Paul. But this may be going too far. What, then, is this criticism of the law that we are talking about?

It is not a criticism of law in the general sense. There is a strain in Western thought that is hostile to law as such. The reasoning runs something like this: laws lay down general principles while reality consists of many specific instances. "Stealing" is an abstract concept because it puts under one heading a whole host of cases which are included in a common class though, in addition to the defining characteristic they have in common, some characteristics are unique to each individual case of stealing. Justice is therefore not done simply by following the law, but by determining what is right in the given situation, and this is an intuitive judgment, requiring the response of the whole person (Buber) or the perception of an indefinable quality not subject to further discussion (G. E. Moore). At best, laws can be approximations or serve as pointers to be taken into consideration among other factors. Such antinomianism, currently represented by situation ethics, is a philosophical criticism of law, just as Kantian ethics is a philosophical defense of law in its purest sense. And, just as Kantian ethics is not Torah (certain nineteenth century Jewish writers to the contrary notwithstanding), so philosophical antinomianism is not a critique of the Torah of Moses, the Torah of Israel's covenant. It need not be denied that some echoes of such philosophical antinomianism may be present in Paul and Luther; in any case, they are not the crux of the matter.

The next attitude to the law, considerably more germane to our purposes than philosophical antinomianism, is the kind we encounter in the Gospels. Examples of this would be Matt. 5:17–20; 12:1–13; 19:1–9; and 15:3–11 (restricting our examples to Matthew for the sake of simplicity). I do not find it very easy to weave even these few passages into a unified doctrine of the law. There are several motifs. One of these is a clear-cut reaffirmation of the law, as in 5:17–19. Indeed, the subsequent "You have heard. . . . But I say to you" formula is easily read as an exercise of the well-established rabbinic function of "building a fence around the law," with the innovation consisting of going beyond the rabbinic fence-building activity toward higher fences, even further removed and therefore more protective of the scriptural prohibition. In this sense, criticism of the law is criticism of rabbinic law or what in Judaism is the oral law. The rabbinic function, as understood within Judaism, was twofold: the transmission and exposition of the divinely revealed interpretation of the written law, and a legislative function whereby rabbinic prohibitions were legislatively added to the biblical ones as a protective measure. At times, Jesus seems to be criticizing only the latter, teaching that it was not applied with sufficient vigor and substituting for it a considerably more vigorous version. At other times, the criticism extends to the rabbinic transmission of the oral law which Jesus finds defective. His arguments, as in 12:3–7, have a talmudic quality because they operate from within the system. It must be remembered that such argument is the very substance of which the Talmud is made. Understood in this sense, the teaching of Jesus is merely another rabbinic opinion among many others. We would then not be dealing with a criticism of "the law" but with one school of thought within the law.

While some of this is undoubtedly the case, there are two reasons why it cannot be the whole truth. I have no firm confidence, even if we restrict our view to Matthew, that Jesus clearly distinguishes between scriptural commandment and rabbinic interpretation. A statement such as "not what goes into the mouth defiles a man, but what comes out of the mouth, this defiles a man" (15:11) relegates too much of the Hebrew Bible to nonimportance. Rabbinic literature is not short on the most emphatic strictures against hateful and venomous speech and on the harm that forbidden speech causes the speaker. But there is too much in Scripture about foods to place it in the realm of the unimportant. That Jesus can do so is understandable to the Jewish reader only in light of the other factor that we cannot omit in this context: the messianic atmosphere of the Gospels. W. D. Davies is the writer who has most cogently drawn our attention to the Jewish sources which intimate a change in the law in messianic times. And while it is true that Davies, as he now agrees, overrated the significance of the rabbinic texts which state or imply the transformation of the law in messianic times, it remains a fact that there is much rabbinic inclination in that direction. That being the case, a good portion of the extralaw atmosphere in the Gospels is explainable by the conviction that the end of days had either come or was very near coming, and that a new Torah was now in effect. Seen from this point of view, we cannot, it seems to me, speak of a critique of the law. The law is or was binding in the period from creation to the advent of the Messiah; from that time on we are dealing with a divine transformation of the human condition and, as part of it, a law appropriate to this new condition.

However vivid the advent of the end of days may have been to Jesus and his followers, however certain they were that their Lord would return for the final act of the drama in their own lifetimes, there seems to be no question that before long the early church had to concentrate its messianic proclamation within the domain of the church, which would continue to exist side by side with an unredeemed world. It is true, of course, that the existence of the island of redemption that was the church qualified the nonredemption of the world, if for no other reason than the possibility given to the individual of leaving the one domain for the other. Nevertheless, the emergence of a non-Jewish church not only alongside an unredeemed world but also alongside an Israel that was not persuaded of the messianic advent for which it continued to hope, makes necessary a critique of the law in the sense in which this culminates in Luther. It will, of course, be clear that Luther's view of the law is related to Paul's, though, I believe, with some differences perhaps not usually sufficiently noticed.

It seems generally agreed that the problem of the law is of central concern to Luther. Not since Paul had a Christian writer been so preoccupied with the law. The reason for this is not difficult to find. Reacting against an atmosphere in which the tradition of the church coexisted in equality—if not more—with Scripture, Luther insists that the word of God in Scripture is the standard by which all teaching is to be measured. When the Bible is taken seriously to this extent, the overwhelming reality of the Old Testament makes itself evident. Alongside the more soteriological texts of the New Testament, the bulk of the Old Testament, with its emphasis on the covenant with Israel and the God of Israel as the giver of the law, is simply too much present to be ignored. How can New Testament soteriology be reconciled with a divine lawgiver as known by Israel? Luther's answer is relatively simple.

The God of the Old Testament is a commanding God who demands action in accordance with his will under the threat of severe punishment. But it is fundamentally not in man's power to obey God's command because man naturally tends in every direction except the one desired by God. As a result, one of two things can happen. In the first case, man deludes himself into believing that he is indeed obeying the law, and that in the process he is building up all sorts of credit with God; thus, he winds up a self-righteous hypocrite who does not even dream of his condemnation in God's eyes, so that the message of Christ, that man's burden of guilt has been lifted, can have no meaning whatsoever for him. The other possibility, though perhaps a bit more to be preferred, is also far from satisfactory. Here the man under the judgment of the law is simply overwhelmed by the magnitude of his guilt and the discrepancy between what he should be and what he is. He is filled with a sense of his weakness and becomes convinced of his inability to extricate himself from the dire situation in which he finds himself. To such a person the gospel of salvation, a salvation not of his own making but the fruit of God's intervention, is meaningful indeed. But without this gospel Luther affirms existence under the law to be either pervasive self-righteousness or hopeless depression, one or the other of which—or perhaps even both—is the fate of man without Christ. The law therefore serves its highest function when it leads man to this impasse from which only Christ can save him. In Luther's words:

> The proper office of the law is to lead us out of our tents and tabernacles, that is to say, from the quietness and security wherein we dwell, and from trusting in ourselves, and to bring us before the presence of God, to reveal his wrath to us, and to set before us our sins.[3]

Because of the law there is sin and because of sin there is a curse, so that all who rely on the law are under a curse (Gal. 3:10). We have now reached the crossroads. If we take one turn we will find ourselves in the domain of Marcion, Gnosticism, and the repudiation of the Old Testament. Hopefully, there is another road which leads to a Christianity which hears the word of God in the Old as well as the New Testament. But the second road should be traveled only by those who are fully aware of where the first leads and do not wish to travel it.

It is not my purpose here to get involved in the discussion of whether Marcion was a Gnostic in good standing, nor indeed of what the precise syndrome that has come to be referred to as Gnosticism is. We need only remind ourselves that some sort of dualism is present in almost all forms of Gnosticism. There is the world which is dark, dreary, and corrupt, the handiwork of some inferior, generally malevolent deity. Into this dark world souls originating in the upper, benevolent region have fallen and they are now prisoners of the world of matter from which they long to escape. Or, in the more serious case, these souls are incapable even of a will to escape because they have fallen so low that their condition of degradation seems desirable to them. In this situation, the fallen soul can be

3. Martin Luther, *Commentary on Galatians* (Philadelphia: Smith, English and Co., 1960). [Cf. the American edition of *Luther's Works* edited by Jaroslav Pelikan and Helmut T. Lehmann, 56 vols. (Concordia, St. Louis and Philadelphia, Fortress, 1955, vols. 25–26; hereinafter cited as *LW*—Ed.].

rescued only by an intervention of the good God, a God who must be distinguished clearly from the evil God of creation. With this scheme in mind, it is simple to identify the Old Testament, with its law and curse, with the world and its evil author, while the world of the New Testament is the redemptive domain of the good God of grace whose intervention is directed toward saving those who are caught in the clutches of the law. Paul flirts with this when he asserts in Gal. 3:19 that the law "was ordained by angels through an intermediary." It is not very difficult to push this one step further and identify the angels who ordained the law and rule this world as standing in opposition to the redemptive God of the New Testament. I detect overtones of such Gnostic dualism in some passages in Luther which pit law against gospel, such as:

> We imagine as it were, two worlds, the one heavenly and the other earthly. In these two places we place two kinds of righteousness, being separate the one from the other. The righteousness of the law is earthly and hath to do with earthly things . . . Christian righteousness is heavenly . . . whereby we mount up above all laws and wars.[4]

And Blackman sums the case up as follows:

> Consider Luther, a much more significant . . . figure than Marcion, who does, however, bear this comparison with him, that he was not a very systematic thinker. Luther contented himself with a distinction of *Deus revelatus* from *Deus absconditus*. By *Deus absconditus* he understood God as capable of wrath, and this was God as he is in himself, *Deus absolutus*, the creator of all things, before whom men must bow in awe and fear. But for Luther there was no question that this was the same God who had revealed himself in Christ as a God of grace. And yet not very deeply below the surface of Luther's thought can be discerned the same dualism which Marcion made no attempt to submerge . . . the dualism between the grace of God and his justice or righteous anger.[5]

Bifurcated in this way, Old and New Testaments came apart, and the God of Sinai is not the God of Jesus. Christianity must then rid itself of the Old Testament, and lest this suggestion strike us as fantastic in this day and age, we need only remind ourselves of Harnack's famous, or rather infamous, pronouncement.

> The rejection of the Old Testament in the second century was a mistake which the great Church rightly refused to make; the retention of it in the sixteenth century was a fatal legacy which the reformation could not

4. Martin Luther, *Commentary on the Sermon on the Mount* (Philadelphia: Lutheran Publishing Society, 1892), p. 225. [Cf. *LW* 21—Ed.]
5. E. C. Blackman, *Marcion, and His Influence* (London: SPCK, 1948), p. 66.

> yet avoid; but for Protestantism since the nineteenth century to continue to treasure it as a canonical document is the result of a lameness which affects religion and the Church.[6]

This is how far things can go.

We must retrace our steps and see what went wrong. Neither Luther nor Paul rejects the Old Testament in the final analysis, and neither refuses to identify the God of the New Testament with the God of the Hebrew Bible. What then are we to make of Paul's curse which hovers over the adherents of the law? I am convinced that if the law is a curse, and only a curse, then Gnosticism and Marcion are unavoidable. This is the matter that we must now examine.

The curse that Paul is referring to in Galatians is, of course, the curse of Deut. 27:15–26. In chapter 27 we are dealing with blessings and curses referred to in 11:26–32 and given in fuller form in chapter 28. There we start with blessings (2–14) and conclude with the curses (15–68). There is set before Israel a momentous option: if Israel is faithful to its covenant and obeys the demands that are the price of the covenant, then it will be the recipient of the blessings; but if Israel is unfaithful to its covenant and walks after its own heart, then it will suffer from the curses. The curse of the law is therefore the curse that results, not from the law, but from disobeying the law. And just as disobeying the law results in the curse, so does obeying it result in the blessing. This is the risk that Israel runs as a result of its election and commitment to obey the demand of God. When it keeps its side of the bargain, God's people is generously rewarded, but when it does not, it is punished. But why then does Paul speak only of the curse and not at all of the blessing—of the consequences of disobedience rather than of obedience?

There are two simple answers to this question. The first is that Paul seems to be convinced of the inevitability of disobedience rather than obedience. Verse 1 of chapter 28 starts with "And if you obey the voice of the Lord your God, being careful to do all his commandments which I command you this day. . . ," and verse 15 starts with "But if you will not obey the voice of the Lord your God or be careful to do all his commandments and his statutes which I command you this day. . . ." Just as these words stand, and I hope I am not being too literal here, one gets the impression that a genuine option is being given, that Israel as a people or the Israelite as an individual can choose one of these two

6. Adolf von Harnack, *Das Evangelium vom Fremden Gott,* 2nd ed. (1924), p. 217. Quoted by Blackman, *Marcion,* p. 122.

courses of action, the consequences of which are vividly spelled out. As I read these texts I get the feeling that this matter of choice is even emphasized, as if the texts were saying: in spite of the momentous nature of these consequences, ranging from the fullest of blessings to the most terrible of curses, it all hinges on Israel's decision. God has placed this fateful choice in Israel's hands. And, almost as if in anticipation of Paul in Rom. 7:18–20—

> For I know that nothing good dwells within me, that is, in my flesh. I can will what is right, but I cannot do it. For I do not do the good I want, but the evil I do not want is what I do. Now if I do what I do not want, it is no longer I that do it, but sin which dwells within me—

we read in Deut. 30:11–14,

> For this commandment which I command you this day is not too hard for you, neither is it far off. It is not in heaven, that you should say, "Who will go up for us to heaven, and bring it to us, that we may hear it and do it?" Neither is it beyond the sea, that you should say, "Who will go over the sea for us, and bring it to us, that we may hear it and do it?" But the word is very near you; it is in your mouth and in your heart, so that you can do it.

The Torah is not hidden, inaccessible, impossible to obey, containing demands beyond the capacity of a creature of flesh and blood. The Torah is near to Israel, as God is near, and it can be obeyed in faithfulness and love. The net result is that we are left with an apparently opaque mystery. Why does Paul emphasize the difficulty of the law, the ease with which it can be violated, and therefore the ease with which the curse can be incurred? Is the answer to be sought in his own experience, in the sense of liberation that was his in Christ, so that his previous, Old Testament-rabbinic existence appears impossibly sinful and unredeemed in contrast? While these considerations, and several others, may have some relevance, I do not think it possible to penetrate to the heart of the matter until we realize that Paul was writing to gentiles.

In my opinion, it is a grave error to read Paul on the law without noticing that the problem that agitated Paul most of his life was the applicability of the law to gentiles. This becomes clear in Acts 15.

Rabbinic Judaism teaches that the Torah, with its commandments, is the result of God's election of and covenant with Abraham. Because the seed of Abraham is to be God's special people, there is prescribed for this people a code of conduct which is by far more rigorous and demanding than what is required of all other peoples. Of these others, God demands adherence to the seven laws of the sons of Noah, roughly corresponding to the list enumerated in Acts 15:20. When a gentile faithfully observes these commandments, he has a place in the world to come and is considered one of the righteous of the nations. The fate of the Jew, on the other hand, is more difficult. Standing in the election of Abraham and the covenant of Sinai, he is a member of "a people holy to the Lord your God" (Deut. 26:19), and is therefore judged by reference to the Torah with its (according to the tradition) six hundred thirteen commandments, instead of the Noachian seven. While presumably the reward is commensurate, so is the punishment detailed in the curse referred to above. The result is that, while conversion to Judaism by means of circumcision and acceptance of the commandments is possible, and accepted with love if the convert-to-be insists (I might add that once the convert converts, he becomes a Jew like all other Jews), it is nevertheless vital that attempts be made to discourage him from embracing the faith of Israel. He is told that as a righteous gentile, obedient to the basic moral law as reflected in the Noachian commandments, he is acceptable to God, and more than acceptable. Why, then, should he embrace the riskier path of Israel? Though the Torah can be obeyed, it is not particularly easy to do so; thus the risk of transgression and its consequences is considerable. Would it not be to his advantage, he is asked, to remain a non-Jew and serve God as such? Only after he insists on traveling the more difficult path is he accepted.

From Acts 15 we learn that in the very young church, there were those who preached that to be saved in Christ, a gentile must be circumcised, accept the yoke of the law, and then escape the punishment that results from sin by faith in Christ. In fact, these people simply added Christ to orthodox Judaism as the sacrifice by means of which the Jew is freed, not from the law, but from the consequence of violating the law. By Christ's "having become a curse for us" (Gal. 3:13), the curse that hovers over those who are subject to the law, should they violate it, is removed. That is why, according to Paul, Jews so desperately need Christ, because, being under the law, they need relief from its sanctions. One might speculate that for the anti-Pauline group of Jewish Christians, the gentiles might not even need Christ since they are not under these dire sanctions; and to the extent that gentiles desire to be in Christ and to be saved by him, they must enter into the covenant of circumcision and obedience to the law as is demanded by rabbinic conversion.

Paul is more traditional than this. He believes that the gentiles, and as he conceives it according to Acts 15 the Jerusalem church as well, ought not to be encouraged to embrace the law (for the reasons indicated previously). If circumcision and obedience to the law is the only way that the gentile can enter the people of God, even after the coming of Christ, then very little has changed, because this was true before Christ as well. What Christ has accomplished, according to Paul, is that now a gentile who obeys the Noachian commandments and believes in Christ, is a member of the new people of God. Through faith in Christ, the wild olive shoot (Rom. 11:17–24) is grafted onto the olive tree, a grafting that before Christ could occur only through circumcision. After Christ, there are two branches to the olive tree, the old and the new. Together they form a unity but not a uniformity. Each retains its identity and its particular obligation. My hypothesis, then, is that for Paul the Jewish-Christian branch of the church, being circumcised, understood itself, and was understood by Paul, to be obligated by the commandments of the Torah. I have no other way of understanding the letter of Acts 15:23–29 and the preceding debate. Surely James would hardly advocate "that we should not trouble those of the Gentiles who turn to God, but should write to them to abstain from the pollutions of idols and from unchastity and from what is strangled and from blood" (Acts 15:19–20) if the Jerusalem church itself believed that with its faith in Christ the Jerusalem Christians were under obligation only to the Noachian commandments instead of the full Mosaic law. The debate of this chapter revolves around what ought to be demanded of gentiles who have come to Christ, whether they must also accept circumcision and the law. But that the Jewish-Christian will continue to do so seems to be taken for granted.

It is true, of course, that my thesis implies, as I have already indicated, that Paul believed in a church with two components: a Jewish one with the Torah and Christ, and a gentile one with the Noachian commandments and Christ. Would this not conflict with Gal. 3:28: "There is neither Jew nor Greek, there is neither slave nor free, there is neither male nor female: for you are all one in Christ Jesus"? Does this not preclude any sort of division within the one church of Christ? I think it precludes only ultimate divisions, but nothing short of the ultimate. Paul counsels women not to speak in the synagogue (1 Cor. 15:34), slaves to be obedient to their masters, and masters to be just to their slaves (Eph. 6:5–9). In the ultimate sense, there are no divisions in the church, and all men, Greek, Jew, master, slave are one in Christ. But this does not abolish the penultimate divisions such as between men and women who, while one in Christ, have their individual roles growing out of their natures, the social order, and the will of God. In the same way, in the ultimate sense, for Paul, the Jewish-Christian and gentile segments of the church are one through their common faith in their savior. But this does not, I think, prevent Paul from thinking of Jewish-Christians as obligated by the commandments of the Torah while this is not true of gentiles who embrace Christ.

One final word before we leave this topic. We asked earlier why Paul speaks only of the curse of the law, not of its blessing, why he speaks of the sins that the law makes possible and not of the obedience which is also made possible. The answer, I think, is simple. Paul is a Jew writing to gentiles whom he is desperately trying to discourage from circumcision and the law. Therefore, just like any rabbi today would, and does under similar circumstances, he stresses to the prospective convert the difficulties and not the opportunities, so as to make his discouragement as discouraging as possible. However significant a portion of the truth this may be, and I have no doubt that it is a significant portion of the truth, it is not the whole truth. For the seed of Abraham the Torah is a covenant of God's love as well as his judgment, a divine word that Israel hears, studies, and sometimes obeys. It is the demand made of Israel by the God who is its covenant partner and loving father. Israel experiences the Torah as demand—but also as gift, so that through its possession Israel is made a holy people and a nation of priests. The terror that overwhelmed Luther as he saw himself crushed by the demands of the law is understandable to the Jew because he is not unacquainted with the reality of the fear of God. At the same time he knows that he is enveloped by a love with which God loves the people of Israel and that demand and love must not be separated.

If what I have said is true, then it follows that Luther misunderstood Paul, reading the apostle's comments about the law, addressed to gentiles and designed to dissuade them from embracing Judaism, as if these comments constituted a full evaluation of the Torah, equally applicable to Jew and gentile. We must be grateful that, Marcion and Harnack notwithstanding, and in spite of this erroneous reading of Paul, the church clung to the Hebrew Bible. And because it did, dialogue between Christians and Jews is possible.

2.

Law and Grace in Judaism and Lutheranism

HORACE D. HUMMEL

To do any sort of justice to this topic in a way relevant to today's dialogue between Jews and Lutherans requires that some attention be paid to both the Old and New Testaments as well as to the variety of developments subsequent to the biblical periods in both Judaism and Christianity (specifically, here, Lutheranism). In these matters I dare claim any kind of scientific, professional competence only with respect to the Old Testament, and in respect to all of them it will be even more evident to others than to myself, no doubt, to what extent my own idiosyncratic viewpoints have intruded.

Having said this, I think it will be plain that I propose to attack the subject more historically than systematically, although many issues will have to be passed over. One axiom obviously presupposed in such an approach is that of underlying unity throughout all the changing forms and accents of these religious developments. (I am personally enamored of John Bright's "evolution outward," as a flower from a bud, to describe the development of certain original, constitutive ideas and impulses.)

The basic bifurcation, of course, comes at the end of the Old Testament era when both Judaism and Christianity sprout from the common trunk of what, for convenience, I shall call Yahwism. (The more technical questions of precisely when one can properly speak of Judaism or of the stages in the development of early Christianity need not detain us here.) Both are in continuity with the common ancestor, but each views its heritage in a different light and interprets it with a different hermeneutic. As we all know, all too early the long night of polemics, misrepresentation, and sometimes plain persecution beclouded the simple disagreements. The basic differences in confession are undoubtedly still with us, but hopefully the time is ripe to try to remove the misunderstandings and misrepresentations that have accumulated.

I

Let us begin our discussion of "law and grace" chronologically with the Old Testament. Various Hebrew words are translatable as "law," "commandment," "statute," "decree," etc., but *torah* is easily the towering term, partly due to inner-biblical developments, partly because of its fateful Septuagintal rendering by *nomos*. In the earlier literature, especially P, *torah* is primarily a specific decision especially of cultic or ritual matters by priests (but with divine authority), and in this sense we often meet it in the plural, *toroth*. That its limited application in P is partly due to the nature of the source may be indicated by its early use by the prophets in a more general sense of divine direction ("the word of God"), and perhaps also in its early Wisdom use as "instruction." That is, as far as we can judge, the laws were meaningful only in the context of the "law" in its more comprehensive sense of revelation, and in any case the very rendering "law" in most translations since the Septuagint invites all sorts of misunderstandings. As I never tire of emphasizing to Christian (and especially Lutheran) audiences, "law" (*torah*) in Old Testament usage is in its whole semantic range quite parallel to "gospel" —and is certainly not its antonym! Apparently, the decisive change in the direction of identifying *torah* with a book comes in Deuteronomy, even though it must also be noted that no other Old Testament work has a more profound understanding than Deuteronomy of the essential grace character of Yahwism, especially in its ethics.

As we turn from problems of vocabulary to issues of substance, we do well to concentrate especially on the Book of Exodus with its account of the exodus and Sinai, followed by a good sampling of "laws," technically of diverse origin, but all obviously related theologically to the preceding events. God had first shown his free, unconditioned grace in the election of Abraham and the promises to him and his descendants, however refractory they might often prove themselves to be. Exodus, Sinai, the conquest, and ultimately the gift of kingship were major stages in the fulfillment of those promises. The covenant was the specific articulation of the grace of election in the here and now where Israel lived and had to exercise her faithfulness. The metaphors were often legal, but the substance was not legalistic. Apart from the election and the gracious promise, covenant had no meaning. If the election was Israel's etiology, and if the promises indicated, under God, where she was going, then the covenant and its laws articulated who she was and how she should respond in the interim. (And this does indeed mean that a certain eschatology was implicit at the outset, however embryonically, in the very terms "covenant" and "law"—an implication which the prophets would later radicalize, and which, according to Christianity's confession, Jesus would, in a sense, radicalize still further.)

Of course, this rough sketch of Israel's *credo* (of God's grace to Israel), to use a term which especially Gerhard von Rad has popularized, could be expanded at much greater length. The strange—indeed, virtually incredible—thing is the unanimity with which almost all current Old Testament scholarship accepts the broad outlines of this picture. To what extent the Israelite confession reflects actual historical events is a serious question on which there is no unanimity. But that, by whatever process and on whatever basis, Israel *did* so confess God's grace as constituting and sustaining her very existence, virtually no one denies.

The only critical questions which need detain us at all are those of the date of that confession and especially the date when all its components were put together into their normative sequence. In the earlier (Wellhausenian) days of criticism, it was fashionable to argue that developed ideas of covenant, law, cultus, etc., were signs of a late, institutionalized, and hence decadent culture. More recently, Martin Noth, von Rad, and others have argued on alleged form-critical grounds for the originally independent origins of the exodus and Sinai (grace and law, if you will) themes, and for their later and artificial welding together under cultic auspices in the period of the Judges. And most recently Gerstenberger and Richter have argued for the earliest origins of both law and wisdom themes in the family or clan, the theological and liturgical motive clauses being added only later. This is not the place to thresh through these issues as such, although I cannot refrain from stressing that weighty arguments can be and have been advanced against those hypotheses, partly on the basis of extrabiblical evidence provided by archaeology.

What is of concern here is the possibility, if not probability, that hidden agendas stand behind many such hypotheses, based on the scarcely recognized biases of their champions. Thus especially G. E. Wright has argued repeatedly that Lutheran assumptions about the separation of law and gospel may underlie the German tendency to separate the exodus and Sinai themes. And, more to the point here, it is hard to escape the suspicion that certain anti-Jewish feelings were a factor in the Wellhausenian conclusions about the lateness and often total nonhistoricity of the priestly source and of many central Old Testament themes (not to speak of his view of Yahweh as basically a God of wrath, uninterested in the individual, etc.). At any rate, confidence in the objectivity of that generation of scholars in this regard is scarcely strengthened when one notes the sometimes subtle—and sometimes quite blatant—anti-Semitism which is repeatedly evidenced in their scholarly writings. Hence, one is scarcely surprised to note the great reserve with which most Jewish biblical scholars have treated the "assured results" of critical orthodoxy, and the generally far higher regard which they have for the antiquity and reliability of the Old Testament traditions. I, for one, have been highly impressed by many of their arguments. And, if it is true that the Jewish scholars here are swayed by a subliminal regard for their only Scriptures, and appear to be exhibiting a last ditch defense against the historical skepticism which Christians tend to reserve for the New Testament (in practice, at least, considering the Old Testament much more dispensable), then, in all fairness, it should also be noted that many Jews—understandably—are much more ready to accept rather uncritically some of the more radical critical conclusions which pit Jesus against Paul and later Christology, than many Christians, at least of the church-oriented and confessionally conscious type, are able to do.

Since the law, however defined, is so often considered to be summarized or typified in the decalogue, we might do well to center our attention there. As virtually everyone knows, there is firm agreement in all traditions that there should be *ten* commandments, but no agreement on just how to distribute the material of Exod. 20 (Deut. 5) into ten units. Not only is Christendom itself split along Lutheran-Roman Catholic and Reformed-Orthodox lines, there is also the traditional Jewish numbering. It seems to me that the Jewish arrangement easily takes the honors if the criterion is, Which one most faithfully reproduces the original spirit and intent? And just because that original spirit and intent tends to be obscured in both of the Christian traditions, we must face the question of which is cause and which effect.

The Jewish tradition, of course, begins its list with Exod. 20:2, "I am Yahweh, your God, who brought you out of the land of Egypt, out of the house of bondage," which is a classical summary of the previous chapters of Exodus, and also a classical statement of how God's grace

had been constitutively revealed to Israel (corresponding quite exactly to the role of the death and resurrection of Christ in the Christian kerygma), so that what follows in the remaining nine is meaningful only in the context of grace, i.e., as response to it, as exhibition of Israel's side of the covenant.

Two other factors in the original text reinforce this exegesis. One of these is also expressed in the Jewish idiom, following Exod. 20:1, which speaks of ten "words" or "sayings," not commandments. Except perhaps indirectly in verse 6 (the close of commandments in Lutheranism's usual rearrangement, and in classical criticism usually attributed to a redactor), that term is not used in Exod. 20 (although it is more prominent in the retrospective form of Deut. 5). I am sure one can make too much out of the slight change in idioms, but for one who is already inclined to view law as opposite to grace, the designation "commandment" will certainly not discourage that misconception. And, as noted above, the omission of verse 2 in the whole Christian tradition, a verse which clearly is no commandment of any sort, will not help either.

Another pointer in the same direction is the grammatical form of the original Hebrew: *lo* with an *indicative*, not *al*, introducing the regular negative command. The "thou shalt" of our archaic English translations or the "you shall" of the recent ones undoubtedly try to reproduce that Hebrew nuance faithfully, but I think that they are rarely heard properly, mostly because of strong prior presumptions to the contrary. (It must be conceded that there is a possibility that the idiom here, as elsewhere sometimes, represents only the imperious, absolute commands of a [divine] monarch, but in this case it seems to me that the entire context argues overwhelmingly against it.) Verse 2 in effect seems to play the role of a conditional clause with respect to what follows: *"If* you know and have experienced my grace (exodus, etc.), *then* you simply *won't* behave in a way that belies your confession, as summarized below." The emphasis is not on coercion or merit, but on prevenient grace, on the spirit, on the spontaneity of the response.

Finally, this exegesis also presupposes a certain understanding of the negative *form* of the commandments, which I think is also quite unanimously shared by contemporary exegetes. Their import is not that of a religion of do's and don'ts. Only a thoroughgoing antinomian and libertine conception of freedom could understand their original intent as restricting man's freedom. On the contrary, the decalogue stands precisely as Israel's charter of freedom (understood as really available only under some authority), stating the *outside limits* beyond which there can be no freedom because authority will have been renounced too. (Though the behavior that establishes a relationship with Yahweh is not commanded, behavior that destroys that relationship is prohibited.) Within those limits as somewhat symbolically summarized in the decalogue, there is to be essential freedom. Hence, there is also the minimal presence here of positive formulations (third and fourth commandments, the former with an infinitive absolute) which indeed leave no alternatives but absolute obedience or disobedience, or some sort of casuistry. (Cf. George Mendenhall, G. Ernest Wright, Gerhard von Rad, Johann Stamm, and Walther Zimmerli.)

What about all the other *toroth*, then, of the Old Testament? Whatever the ultimate, technical origins of both apodictic and casuistic law, and whatever the various literary sources where these types were collected, it is undeniable that *theologically* all have been brought into intimate relationship with the exodus and Sinai events, as is shown alone by the fact that they follow hard on Exod. 20, and as reaffirmed by Deuteronomy in its own unique way. Within the Old Testament context itself (i.e., before the later compulsion to harmonize), the very hiatuses, varying degrees of completeness, and other inconsistencies (many of them probably reflecting historical or geographical variations) indicate to what extent *toroth* are representative and illustrative rather than exhaustive, legalistic codes. Formally, I think they can be compared with the Sermon on the Mount or the evangelical counsels at the end of many Pauline letters which illustrate eschatological existence in Christ or the third use of the law, to which we turn shortly.

Perhaps one other observation is in order here, which may also serve as a transitional device. One factor which has long befouled Jewish-Christian relations (and of which the Six Day War and other aspects of the Arab-Israeli conflict have sharply reminded us) is the difficulty Christians have in grasping the fact that Judaism is not and cannot be simply another "religion" in the same sense that the term applies to Christianity. That is, Judaism is inextricably related (somehow!) to concerns of land, peoplehood, and cult (as well as of theology and ethics), which can simply not be predicated of Christianity. And if this is true of modern Judaism, it is surely true *a fortiori* of ancient Israel as a nation among the nations, who had received her *land* as a fundamental part of the patriarchal blessing. Hence Israel is to respond faithfully to her redeemer's grace not only in the realm of spirituality, not only in individual and social ethics, but also in liturgy, agriculture, jurisprudence, and statecraft, etc. In the nature of the case, in these areas, mere generalized ideals will not quite suffice. But also here the note of freedom should not be lost sight of: Israel does not *basically* need to torment herself with the question of how to be faithful in the manifold aspects of living: God has *freed* her from that, by indicating with what he is pleased and how his will is to be done.

Thus, who could be surprised at the refrain of *simchath Torah* which resounds so loudly and eloquently wherever in the Old Testament, and especially in the Psalter, we are allowed to hear the congregation's own response to the *magnalia Dei* ("great works of God")?

II

In the post-Old Testament period, let us first try to sketch developments in the Jewish community after the exile. I think now we can begin to speak of "Judaism" in contrast to Yahwism, although it is debatable just how one should date a very gradual shift (at the time of Ezra? Hillel and Shammai?), and the Talmud will not be completed for several centuries yet. But, it is plain that in New Testament times halakic and haggadic interpretations were flourishing, the Tannaim were active, and the Pharisaic party from which normative Judaism would develop was fast establishing itself.

Concerning shifts with respect to *torah,* I think it behooves most Christians to lean over backwards to try to correct a canard which they have often nourished: that Judaism no longer recognized the grace inherent in the law and covenant of Yahwism (assuming that Christians will even concede its presence in the Old Testament itself—sometimes a condition contrary to fact) and hence had become simply a religion of works or merit, in contrast to Christianity which was now the sole possessor of salvation by grace. I am anything but a specialist in Jewish religious literature, either of that time or of today, but even the most cursory acquaintance with that literature, or with Jewish religious life through the ages, must cause one to dismiss such a caricature out of hand. I would happily dismiss it with that, except for knowledge of the fact that it is a notion deeply rooted in the Christian subconscious. Further, it does not find support in the New Testament.

At this point we should note, too, the minimal role which anything comparable to Christian dogmatics or systematics plays in the Jewish tradition. This Christians tend to find highly frustrating. They forget to what an extent this is also true of the biblical literature itself, and what grave weaknesses as well as strengths their own beloved systems exhibit, of which law/gospel is surely a parade example. This unsystematic nature of the Jewish literature makes it quite possible to find certain statements which by themselves sound frightfully legalistic, canceling out grace by their accent on merit, if the countervailing statements extolling and exploring God's grace are neglected. Here, compare New Testament statements—even in Paul!—on *reward* of grace.

Before we leave Judaism, we cannot fail to note that its history contradicts a frequent caricature of it becoming an ever-accumulating casuistry, and hence of an evermore restricted life. That the "spirit who gives freedom" was not forgotten in the history of Judaism is evidenced, among others, in the midrashim, the Qabbalistic literature, the Hassidic movements, Reform and Conservative Judaism, and perhaps even the often militant "anti-ghetto" secularism of much of modern Israel.

At the same time, however, that we insist that the centrality of grace in Yahwism by no means disappeared in Judaism, it must also be asserted that, beginning with the Babylonian exile, a number of developments did easily obscure, at least in practice, the more radical emphasis on grace in the Mosaic covenant, as reaffirmed by the prophets. We see this in the increasing tendency to consider the law as something absolute, preexistent, timeless, to which God himself is virtually subject, and of which Moses was only a rather passive middleman. We see it in the facile identification of law with the Pentateuch (or the rest of the canon viewed as quite strictly subordinate to it) and as something which "defiles the hands" (is sacrosanct and inerrant). We see it in the increased emphasis on what *separates* the Jew from the gentile, on the necessity to *keep* the law in order to obtain life, and the apparent assumption that in principle the law *can* be kept. One certainly has no difficulty understanding many of these emphases in the context of the time, and most of them probably *can* be understood theologically in a way which does not clash with grace. But their very one-sidedness easily led to caricatures of the original intent of the Mosaic Torah. It is possible that the New Testament also one-sidedly scores these developments because of its apologetic concerns, but I do not think it can be denied that they *did* exist, whatever one's ultimate valuation of them.

III

In the New Testament the overarching unity to be borne in mind, without which nothing will be clearly understood, is that of its *eschatological* point of departure. Beginning with such passages as Jer. 31 which looked forward to the new covenant to be established beyond the judgment by a new, free act of God (and a host of similar passages, especially as interpreted in apocalyptic light), the New Testament proclaimed above all that Jesus of Nazareth *was* the Messiah, that the kingdom of God *had* come near, and that the new aeon *had* broken in. On such confessions the Christian church still stands or falls. I doubt that the fundamental issues are ultimately any different now from what they were in the first century of the Common Era. To remove, however, some of the mutual misunderstandings and caricatures which have developed would be no small accomplishment.

If we begin with and understand this eschatological viewpoint, it will be clear that the New Testament's interests are *theological*, not ethnic. That is, assertions that the New Testament is an anti-Semitic book will be seen as thoroughly indefensible. This is not to say, of course, that it could not be so misunderstood and misused. It obviously often has been. Nor do I think it will be found true that the New Testament even misunderstands or basically misrepresents Judaism (not even Paul), although again the apologetic and/or polemical concerns of the writers will have to be borne in mind. Neither, then, do I think we will allow ourselves to be sidetracked by the specific *proof texts* or *testimonia* used to prove the Christian confession. The Qumran evidence seems to indicate that, in general, the hermeneutics employed in the New Testament had more in common with the eschatological method of the Essenes than with that of the main line rabbinical interpreters. But in either event the New Testament hermeneutic was not, like modern exegesis, primarily concerned to reproduce what the text originally meant. Rather it was concerned with what it meant in light of the ongoing actualization of God's grace, or in the light of the dawn of the eschaton, as the case might be.

When one examines the New Testament concepts of fulfillment, newness, and antitype (themselves formally taken from the Old Testament), one notes first of all that they include aspects *both* of continuity and of discontinuity. They both affirm and negate the old, and here specifically, the Torah. Jesus has come "not to destroy, but to fulfill the law" (Matt. 5:17). He himself keeps the law *perfectly* for the first time, and his very criticism of the law is really intended as an affirmation of its deepest intent, now available as a free gift in baptism through him for all who will accept it.

The two tables of the law are still summarized by the New Testament in Old Testament quotations: (1) love God with all your heart, etc. (Deut. 6:5—following hard upon the *shema*); and (2) love your neighbor as yourself (Lev. 19:18). But the New Testament's sense of fulfillment in Jesus also brings with it a heightened sense of sin, and then of the need for total dependence upon God's grace. What is "bad" about the old is not intrinsic, but occurs because the old has been superseded and fulfilled by the new. He who clings to the old is culpable only because, if you will, he has not moved along with God into the final stage of the process of redemption.

These points have to be made especially with respect to St. Paul, not only because the early conflict with Judaism and the "Judaizers" is seen most sharply in him, but also because his language provides the point of departure for so many Lutheran formulations about the "law." Again, I think it cannot be reaffirmed too strongly that Paul has no intention of describing what the *torah* meant *before* the advent of Christ, but what it means *now*. His exegesis is totally theological, not historical as we understand the term today. Only in that light can we make sense of Paul's accent on the *curse* of the law; on man's total inability to keep its demands; on the negative form of the decalogue; on his insistence that the Jew who recoils from the christological climax is "without excuse" before God as much as the gentiles; and, almost shockingly, only in this light can we understand that for Paul the *torah* can *now* even be equated with the "elemental spirits of the universe" (Gal. 4, Col. 2), i.e., that the Jewish faith is no better than all the other religions and schemes of redemption which reject Christ crucified and risen again. If all of this is not seen as eschatological exegesis, it certainly clashes head on with *torah* as conceived and presented in the Old Testament.

But we dare not leave St. Paul without also noting his many affirmative statements about the law, and indicating that he means to proclaim the aspects of continuity of the *pleroma* ("fulness") as much as other New Testament writers. Especially to be noted are such passages as the typology of 1 Cor. 10, Rom. 7 ("the law is holy"), and, above all, Rom. 9–11. Especially in the Pauline corpus, the latter chapters provide a much needed balance to grasp the entirety of Paul's thought. It is regrettable that Christian exegesis has neglected or skirted them as much as it has. All details aside, they make crystal clear that any and all formulations about Jews as a people now accursed and rejected by God, "Christ-killers" and what not, are simply incompatible with Pauline (and any genuinely Christian) thought. Furthermore, in some sense Paul makes plain that the Jews are still the "people of God," and the ancient covenant with them has not been revoked in spite of their failure to convert. Where we go from there is not so clear, and perhaps we must leave it where Paul does, as part of the mystery of the economy of salvation, which God controls, not we, Jews or Christians.

IV

Let us finally take a look at Lutheranism and its relationship both to the above survey of the biblical evidence and to the question of Jewish-Lutheran dialogue. Now, it is quite well known that Paul was one of Luther's and Lutheranism's favorite biblical writers, so much so that Lutheranism has sometimes been accused of making the rest of the Bible, even the rest of the New Testament, deuterocanonical. There is no denying that in all types of confessionally based Lutheranism, law/gospel has always been one of the dominant and central themes, although there have been variations in accent and proportion.

I should make it very plain that I speak as one who for the most part has nothing but the highest regard for theology oriented in the direction of confessionally based Lutheranism. I am convinced that it intends to be totally faithful to what is central to Scripture, and is, in fact, a major safeguard toward that end. At the same time, it easily becomes idolatrous to act as though any formulation or phraseology completely captures all the variety within Scripture or is incapable of profound abuse. It has been one of the signal contributions of the late "biblical theology" movement to remind us of the difference between biblical usages and those of later dogmatics, of which there is no better example than "law."

Even the classical dogmatic tradition speaks of *three* "uses" of the law. To a certain extent this is also true of many other traditions besides the Lutheran. (1) The "first use" of the law, the *usus politicus,* describes God's lordship over all creation and all mankind, evil or good, which is normally delegated by God to duly constituted human authority as a curb in order to maintain law and order, and justice, on earth. (2) The "second use," *usus elenchthicus*, is that mirror use by which God confronts man with his holy and absolute demands and convicts man of his inability to meet them internally and perfectly, and thus teaches man to be utterly dependent upon grace (following Paul). (3) The "third use," *usus didacticus*, is that "rule" by which God suggests and guides concrete obedience even for the converted man who "walks by the Spirit."

When Lutherans speak of law without further qualification, it is normally (following Paul) the "second use" which is meant (hence, the priority given to the decalogue in Luther's two catechisms). *Lex semper accusat*, "the law always accuses." This second use exposes the invalidity before God of all views of the law which assume that by obedience to the law or by "being sincere and doing his best," man can accumulate merit before God and supplement grace or even make it superfluous.

With this kind of theology I am in the heartiest agreement, but all kinds of problems arise when two things are forgotten: (1) the eschatological viewpoint from which Paul writes, and, hence, (2) the very specialized way in which he and the dogmatic tradition use the term "law." I think it is demonstrable that Luther and the first generation after him were also eschatologically conscious and hence reproduced the dynamic of the Pauline term relatively faithfully. However, as this dynamic faded in later generations and hardened into a system, the term "law" itself almost became a static absolute. In some respects, it is a striking parallel to what had occurred in the early rabbinic period. In fact, it was probably the Achilles heel and one of the great ironies of the whole edifice of Lutheran Orthodoxy that it was founded on an essentially legalistic (rationalistic) understanding of law as an objective eternal scheme of demands and prohibitions. In more recent time, as I read the works of the great exponents of law/gospel such as Werner Elert (to whose writings I am greatly indebted) I am shocked to see what terminological difficulty even such a giant as he has in perceiving the difference in usage between Old Testament *torah* and Pauline *nomos*. The former becomes basically just a foil to the latter, and Yahwism must be understood as a fundamentally different religion, one based on merit, not grace. Thus one can scarcely be surprised when such quasi-Lutheran systems as those of Rudolph Bultmann, Friedrich Baumgaertel, and their congeners drive home such fundamental misunderstandings of the Old Testament with a vengeance.

Such negativistic views of the Old Testament may or may not be transferred to Judaism, but the extent to which the "German Christians" in Nazi Germany also wanted to expunge the Old Testament from the Christian canon reminds us of the close potential connection between the two. Already in Luther one stumbles across statements which, taken by themselves, come perilously close to a simple identification of "law" in the Pauline sense with the Old Testament. However, these are so balanced by Luther's christological interpretation that the positive element of spiritual continuity easily dominates. That raises other questions which we cannot entertain here, but it does remind us of the extent to which Christianity's own integrity is involved. As Wright repeatedly emphasizes, if the New Testament is not the fulfillment of the promises given in the Old Testament, then it can only be the fulfillment of man's own hopes and ideals however he chooses to define them (perhaps also of keeping the Aryan race *judenrein*—"free of Jews"). In broader terms, then, Christianity should not be unconscious of its direct debt to Jewish biblical scholarship in keeping the Old Testament alive in its own midst.

In contrast to Lutheranism, the Reformed tradition has always put greater stress on the "third use" of the law, to which corresponds the far greater use which Old Testament ethics, covenant terminology, and psalmody have played in the Calvinistic ethos, and, conversely, the deep Lutheran suspicions, often prevailing even today, of any kind of *Heilsgeschichte* theology. It remains to be seen to what extent the ecumenical era will succeed in harmonizing or burying those deeply rooted differences. Within Lutheranism itself, many a logomachy has raged around the question of whether one can even properly speak of a third use of the law. What need does he who has been ushered into eschatological existence in Christ have of laws or rules in any sense? (Cf. Augustine's "Love God, and do whatever you please" and similar statements in Luther.)

Another hermeneutical question arises here concerning the nature of New Testament eschatology ("realized," "futuristic," or what?). I think Oscar Cullmann's answer is easily the most faithful to the biblical evidence: in the New Testament we meet *both* the "already" or "now" of christological finality and simultaneously (in dialectical tension) the "not yet" of continued hope until the consummation. Thus, Christian ethics is an "interim ethics," its theology is a *theologia viatorum* ("theology of people on the way"), and only in this context are such concepts as Spirit, church, and sacraments theologically meaningful.

But to say that we still exist in the "not yet" is another way of saying that we also still live in the Old Testament era. As part of the Christian canon, the Old Testament speaks to our B.C.-ness (as the New Testament literature also does, when seen from a certain aspect). Such a formulation can be developed in terms of all three "uses" of the law: (1) as we are reminded of our creaturely status; (2) as we are reminded of our sinful status; and (3) as we are reminded (all terminological questions aside) that since we are *simul iustus et peccator* we, at very best, still need guidelines or outside limits by which to order our daily lives in the face of concrete realities. Such a confession of continued imperfection need by no means clash with christological grace.

Otherwise, as noted above, the various ethical guidelines in the New Testament are at best highly superfluous, if not, especially in the case of Paul, self-contradictory. Many have argued correctly that the New Testament does not contain more of such material, partly because of its predominant emphasis on the "now" (although toward the end of the New Testament one notes increasing attention to the manifold "not yet" problems of church order, practical ethics, etc.), and partly because the New Testament evidently did consider it superfluous to *repeat* the many guidelines laid down in the Old Testament, which long remained its sole canon. As the "Israel according to the Spirit," it no longer was obliged to obey those guidelines so directly as God had formerly required; inasmuch as it still was "Israel" (still within the "not yet") the theological intent of those guidelines (response to grace, now *a fortiori*) was still valid, and their concrete suggestions were to be implemented as much as feasible.

I submit that if this whole line of thought were more alive among Lutheran theologians, Lutheranism would not only find its Old Testament more meaningful, but would also, up to a point, experience more empathy with the Jewish concern to be faithful to the Torah. In this connection, Lutherans also need to reexamine their glib, traditional formula that "the Old Testament moral laws remain valid for Christians, but not the ceremonial and political ones." Not only are there questions here about the meaning of law, but also it should be noted that the Old Testament's unitary view of life, with the inseparability of all types of laws, clashes sharply with the implication of a facile dichotomy between spirit and the concrete problems of liturgy and existence in the *polis*.

My final observation, then, would be that while none of the three dogmatic uses of law correspond to *torah* in the Old Testament, all three agree in substance with aspects of Old Testament theology (and *a fortiori* of the New Testament).

(1) That Yahweh is creator and king of the universe is part of the bedrock of both Yahwism and Judaism and that he delegates his author-

ity to the nations and holds them morally responsible, his special relationships to Israel notwithstanding, is repeatedly articulated (Deut. 32:8; Ps. 82—the prophetic "gentile oracles," etc.).

(2) That God is judge of and will judge all creation is also prominent. This is really the point of the protology of Gen. 1–11; man's *hybris* and quest for truth ends in a blind alley, so that God's consequent will in the election of Israel is man's only hope of escape from the comprehensive judgment. All history, if you will, is thus bracketed in a law/gospel framework; "*die Weltgeschichte ist das Weltgericht*" ("world history is world judgment"). The story of the interim (in a lesser sense than in the New Testament) ends only in the eschatological final judgment. Again, this implies a clear continuity in Old Testament eschatology, in spite of later developments, especially at the hand of apocalyptism. As the initial grace of election was the aftermath of the "final judgment" in the deluge and at the tower of Babel, so the eschatological judgment will usher in the new heavens and the new earth. The Old Testament also knows clearly that "judgment begins with the household of God" (1 Pet. 4:17), i.e., that God sustains his people by a special law/gospel relationship. Is not this the import of the "curse of law," classically expressed in the antiphony of Deut. 27–28, or in P's accent on that almost impersonal wrath which flashes when the sphere of the holy is violated? This insight was made even more radical by the prophets with their prediction that, in order to save Israel, not only wicked *parts* of Israel would have to be punished, but Israel itself would have to go under before the "new covenant" could be established. (Here, see the traditional "alteration of weal and woe" in many collections of prophetic *logoi,* and the common outline of many prophetic books: judgment on Israel, then on the *goyim,* followed by salvation for the "remnant" of all.)

(3) Concerning the "third use" of the law, that God's people, although free from the curse, still need guidance and do not serve him in arbitrary, self-appointed channels, is the point of much of Exod. 20 ff.

Maybe this is not the place to insist parenthetically that (1) the *lex talionis* ("law of retribution") in its Pentateuchal setting is *not* an encouragement of legalistic retribution (cf. Matt. 5:38 and its *eschatological* viewpoint) but is an expression of *restraint* when in the world of power, retaliation seems necessary; and (2) that the imprecatory psalms and holy war must also be understood in the *covenant* context of God's work, and not of purely private or nationalistic vengeance. Since misrepresentations of these points continue to appear regularly in church publications, and often imply aspersions on the whole Old Testament, here we could stand some intelligent "censorship."

Where does *torah,* as used in the Old Testament as general counterpart to gospel, fit into this threefold dogmatic scheme? *Nowhere,* in the sense that *torah* is not equivalent to any of three dogmatic uses of law any more than gospel is. But in another sense, *everywhere*, to those within the covenant. In terms of the chronology of salvation, *torah*, like gospel, must in a sense be assumed as appearing after the "second use" and before the "third use." In another sense, the ultimate import of all three uses remains hidden outside the grace of revelation; none will automatically lead behind the masks of the *Deus absconditus.*

That is to say, in conclusion, that the law/grace structure in the two testaments (i.e., in Judaism and Christianity) is profoundly similar; the issues which divide do not lie here as such, but in the question of the full contours of the grace of the *Deus revelatus.*

3.

Election and the People of God: Some Comments

NILS A. DAHL

1. In traditional Lutheran theology, the theme of election has mainly been treated in the context of the problems of predestination and free will. Being justified by faith alone, man should trust God's election in Christ Jesus, thus avoiding both *superbia* ("pride") and *desperatio* ("hopelessness").

2. The idea of the church as the people of God has been stressed mainly in reaction against the hierarchic structure of the Roman Catholic church, and in some circles in reaction against state church establishments. The connection between the two themes, election and the people of God, would seem in Lutheranism to have been less organic than in Calvinistic and Puritan tradition. This may possibly be one reason for the contrast between the American sense of mission and the German notion of the *Eigengessetzlichkeit* ("autonomy") of politics, combined with less disguised forms of nationalism and even racism. (A parenthetical question: Was the background of New England Protestantism one factor which made it possible for G. F. Moore to draw a sympathetic picture of the "revealed religion" of Tannaitic Judaism?)

3. Lutheranism is a faction of the Western part of Christendom, and classical Lutheran theology has been shaped within the framework of Western, post-Augustinian Christianity, in continuation of and contradiction to theological traditions within this part of the church. A conversation with Jewish scholars forces Lutheran theologians to reflect upon biblical themes and contemporary issues to which less than sufficient attention has been paid in the main stream of Lutheran theology.

4. A dialogue between Jews and Christians is complicated by the fact that problems are involved at several levels:

a. Interpretation of texts and understanding of past history. On this level critical methods of research provide a common ground.

b. Contact between representatives of separate traditions and communities, both in some way claiming to be the people of God and heirs of election. A long history of controversies, and ultimate questions of faith, are in the background if not in the forefront of our discussions.

c. Jews and Christians alike have to face the questions of how to preserve—or reshape— the traditions and how to interpret their sacred Scriptures in an age in which the biblical notion of a sovereign God, who chooses and rejects, has become alien and obsolete to a large number of people, even inside the synagogues and churches. Of these sets of questions, which can hardly be kept completely separate from each other, the first one may be the least important but yet provide the best point of departure for reflections.

I

5. In the Hebrew Scriptures, the Old Testament of the church, the notion that Israel is the people of Yahweh (and Yahweh the God of Israel) is much more widespread and central than the specific terminology of election. Explicit statements about God's election of Israel are mainly to be found in Deuteronomy and Second Isaiah (e.g., Deut. 4:37; 7:6 ff.; 14:2; Isa. 41:8 f.; 43:10; 44:1 f., etc.). The idea of the chosen king seems to be older than the idea of the election of a whole nation, and was more common in the ancient Near East than the idea of the chosen people.

6. Reading the books of the Old Testament in their canonical form and in retrospect, one may nevertheless say that the whole biblical story from the creation of the world to the conquest of Canaan and later, although compiled from various traditions and sources, is dominated by one theme: God, who created the world, called Abraham, brought Israel out of Egypt, gave the law at Sinai, and brought the Israelites into the promised land in order that they should be his chosen people, his own possession and a holy nation, keeping his covenant, observing his commandments, and worshiping him at the place of his choice, with a chosen king and a chosen priesthood.

7. The idea of God's choice of a particular people for himself is characteristic of the combination of universal (generally human) and particular (specific) elements which is, in manifold variations, to be found in all the writings of the Old and the New Testaments. (Compare, by contrast, the way in which Greek philosophers tended to find a divine

unity within, or behind, the manifoldness of the world, by way of generalization and abstraction from all particular phenomena.)

8. Only some aspects of the theme election and the people of God in the Old Testament Scriptures can be mentioned here. A Lutheran theologian may be allowed first of all to stress the emphasis put upon God's sovereignty and his faithfulness. The God who chose Israel is both the "jealous God" and is "merciful and gracious, abounding in steadfast love and faithfulness." His freedom over against the people of his preference is especially stressed by the prophets of doom. Judgment and catastrophes are announced, not in spite of, but because of Israel's status as God's people (cf. Amos 3:2 f.). Yet, the last word is a word of God's faithfulness, at least in the canonical books of the prophets.

9. Election is election for a purpose and a function. By stressing the idea of election for service, however, one may easily be in danger of modernizing. Even the task of being witnesses to the Lord is hardly to be understood as primarily a service to the world of nations; the image of "witness" is that of a lawsuit in which the Israelites bear testimony to their God (Isa. 43:10; cf. v. 21). Yet, within the total perspective of Scripture we do find the idea that the particularity of election serves the universality of revelation and salvation (cf. Isa. 2:1–4; 49:5 f.; 51:4 f.).

10. Chosen by God, Israel has to choose either life and good, or death and evil (Deut. 30:15). The people of God have to face the alternative of either blessing or curse. Election is both a privilege and a burden, as exemplified most clearly by Jeremiah and by the servant of the Lord in Second Isaiah.

11. The story of the fathers and the people is presented with a most remarkable realism, without idealization. The sinfulness of the Israelites may in the biblical materials be stressed to the extreme. For this reason, the Old Testament could provide an arsenal of arguments used by Christians in anti-Judaic polemics insofar as Israel is represented as a nation that is holy and sinful at the same time. In later writings, say from Ben Sira onward, there is a greater tendency to present the ancestors as heroes of piety—thus the Apocrypha, pseudepigrapha, and rabbinic literature, but hardly the Prayers of the Synagogue.

12. The question of who belongs to the people of God is to some extent an open one (Judah over against Joseph in Ps. 78:67–68; the concept of the remnant). A contrast between those "who forsake the Lord" and those whom God calls "my chosen" and "my servants" is made in Isa. 65:8 ff. Later on, the Qumran covenanters claimed to be

"the elect of God," "the congregation of his elect," representing the true Israel. On the other hand, gentiles may be given access and nations may be expected to join the Lord and thus become his people (Isa. 56:3–8; Zech. 2:11).

II

13. The early Christians thought themselves to be "a chosen race, a royal priesthood, a holy nation," to use the terminology of 1 Pet. 2:9, derived from Isa. 43:20 and Exod. 19:5 f. Similar claims were made by the people at Qumran, and possibly by other Jewish groups. The application of predicates of Israel to the Christians, however, was not based upon a return to the true interpretation and faithful observation of the Torah, but upon God's vindication of the crucified Messiah, Jesus.

14. Whereas Israel as the chosen people is the preferred, "choice" nation, election in the New Testament is inseparable from being redeemed—in Christ—from a status of being alienated from God, and of being under the sway of sin and death, to the eschatological kingdom of God. Differences of emphasis concerning the relation between divine election and human decision are to be seen as consequences of a basic divergence in the understanding of what is the redemptive act of God. There is no uniform answer to the problem of predestination and/or synergism either in Judaism or in Christianity.

15. While the Christian church claims to be the heir of the promises granted to Israel, the designation "Israel" is, with few exceptions, reserved in the New Testament for the nation of Israel in past and present. The attitude of the earliest communities is likely to be reflected in what Paul writes in Rom. 15:8 f.: "Christ became a servant to the circumcised to show God's truthfulness, in order to confirm the promises given to the patriarchs, and in order that the gentiles might glorify God for his mercy." At the early stage, conversion of the gentiles was an object of eschatological hope more than of missionary efforts. (An early Hebrew Christian "midrash" may be preserved in Gal. 3:13–14*a*; here the crucifixion of Jesus is interpreted as effectuating the promise given to Abraham after the "binding of Isaac" by redeeming the Israelites from the curse inflicted by their transgressions of the law, in order that the blessing of Abraham might, as a consequence, come upon the gentile nations in his "offspring," the Messiah, Jesus.)

16. Paul's ministry and theology were based upon the conviction, which once had made him a persecutor, that the validity of the law and

faith in the crucified Messiah were mutually exclusive. Called to become an apostle, he had to surrender all his privileges as a Jew and identify himself with "gentile sinners," in order to be "justified by faith in Jesus Christ." In order to "uphold" the law as part of Scripture he (re)interprets it in terms of the principle "life by doing" (Lev. 18:5), and contrasts it with the principle "life by faith" (Hab. 2:4. The contradiction arises because "faith" is understood as faith in the crucified Jesus!). Thus Paul finds a conflict between the promise to Abraham and the Mosaic laws, and resolves the conflict by the theory that the holy law was valid for the premessianic time only, intended not to give life but to increase sin.

17. More directly related to the theme of election is another apparent contradiction in Scripture: the God of Israel is at the same time the "king of the nations" and "the God of all flesh" (Jer. 10:7 and 32:27; cf. Rom. 3:29). Here Paul comes up with a new solution to a problem that did not pass unrecognized by rabbinic scholars. "There is no distinction between Jew and Greek," he says. And yet, "the gifts and the call of God [to Israel] are irrevocable" (Rom. 10:12; 11:28). As Paul sees it, the Jews who believe in Christ are "a remnant, chosen by grace." The ministry to the gentiles and their acceptance of the gospel will, he hopes, provoke his kinsmen to jealousy. Seeing both the free sovereignty and the faithfulness of God at work, the apostle warns gentile believers against false security and haughtiness towards those who are by nature branches of the precious "olive tree" (Rom. 9–11).

18. Other New Testament writers deal in different terms with the interrelations between the church and Israel. The author of Ephesians (a Jew who had become a disciple of Paul?) calls Christians of gentile origin to consider what a great mystery it is that Christ has made them "fellow heirs, joint body, and joint partakers of the promise." Luke stresses the fulfillment of the promises given to the fathers and pertaining both to the people of Israel and to the gentile nations; he is anxious to make it clear that Paul was not a Jewish apostate but was under arrest "because of the hope of Israel." Matthew restricts the earthly mission of Jesus to Israel but considers the church of Jews and gentiles another "nation," to which the kingdom of God has been given in order that it should produce the fruits of the kingdom by observing what Jesus had taught his disciples. It is emphasized that even those who confess Jesus as Lord will be judged according to their works; the saying, "Many are called, but few are chosen," is used as a warning in this context.

19. The harsh words against "the Jews" in the Fourth Gospel are linked up with a peculiar doctrine of election. Jesus' initiative in choosing his first disciple is understood as a symbol for what happens to later believers (John 15:16); but even among the twelve there was a traitor. When confronted with Jesus and his word a man shows—sooner or later—what kind of man he is, whether or not he is "of the truth" and belongs to the "sheep" who heed the voice of the Good Shepherd. Israel is understood as being in the center of the world: "Salvation comes from the Jews"; the "other sheep, that are not of this fold," are to be gathered in and united with the disciples of Jesus within Israel. On the other hand, the Jews are the representatives of the world in its opposition to Jesus and, as the evangelist sees it, to God who sent him; only those who had the law could hold that Jesus was guilty and deserving of death because he made himself the Son of God.[1]

20. The simplistic doctrine that Israel was rejected and the church chosen to be a new people of God is not really found within the New Testament, although it is adumbrated in some of the late writings. In vital issues of practical importance there is a good deal of unanimity: The Holy Scriptures are retained and interpreted as warranting the existence of the church as legitimate heir to the promises. Gentiles are admitted as full members of the church. The commandments of the law are regarded as valid only, or mainly (Matthew?), insofar as they are summarized in the commandment(s) of love. But the theology by means of which all this is justified, including both interpretation of Scripture and doctrines about election and the people of God, varies from one writer to the other. This state of affairs is in some respects similar to what we can find in Tannaitic Judaism: various rabbis agree upon what is valid halakah (law and tradition), but find exegetical justification for it in a number of different ways.

III

21. One should not oppose Christian "universalism" to Jewish "particularism." In Christianity, as in Judaism, the doctrines of election and

1. As shown by James Louis Martyn (*History and Theology in the Fourth Gospel* [New York: Harper & Row, 1968]), the Fourth Gospel seems to presuppose the same, or a similar state of controversy between Jews and Christians as the one reflected in the earliest Jewish evidence concerning Jesus and his disciples. The way in which the Fourth Gospel speaks about the Jews may, indeed, promote anti-Semitism, if read and reproduced without any deeper historical and theological understanding.

the people of God imply a combination of universal and specific elements. To Christianity, what is specific is concentrated in the one Jesus Christ; other particular concepts, like the one Mosaic law, the chosen place, or the chosen nation have lost the significance they have had in Judaism. The tendency to regard the church as the new people of God, chosen from the gentiles, and to expect Jews who were baptized to abandon the Jewish way of life marked the beginnings of a specifically gentile Christian form of particularism. The relationship between Christians and Jews in the first centuries of the Christian era, however, must have been more complex than what has often been assumed,

22. The "victory" of Christianity through the Constantinian settlement, followed by adoption of Christianity as the official religion of the Roman Empire, and later of European states, profoundly changed the situation. What had been theological arguments in the rivalry between one persecuted minority group and another was turned into an ideology of the establishment. The Jews were tolerated (almost privileged since pagans were denied the right to practice their religion and even to exist), but discriminated against. Theological concepts like election and the people of God were misused as rationalizations of hostile attitudes and actions toward the Jews, and even inspired such attitudes and actions. The fate of the Jewish people may be the strongest proof of the fragility of the post-Constantinian synthesis, judged by New Testament standards.

23. Luther opposed the power structure of the Roman church as well as a theology of glory. But the Reformation remained within the framework of established Western Christendom, post-Augustinian in theology and post-Constantinian in social and political aspects. The gospel was rediscovered as the true treasure of the church, but was mainly related to the troubled conscience of the individual. In some respects, the social structure of the churches became more than ever conformed to the civil society of "Christian nations," in which Jews were at the best allowed to exist as second-rate citizens. (Jews had no access to the Lutheran kingdom of Norway until the 1840s!) The Pauline doctrine of justification by faith was cherished, but the correlate principle of "no distinction" was never fully envisaged and certainly not effectuated. All warnings against self-righteousness did not affect the deep-rooted Christian self-righteousness over against the Jews. Full appropriation of the biblical witness to God's sovereignty and faithfulness in election, both of Israel and of gentiles, has remained an unresolved task.

24. The amelioration of the status of the Jews, and of the relations

between Jews and Christians, has to a large extent been a result of the ongoing process of secularizing. To some degree, secularization has been a consequence of the Reformation. Luther stressed the dignity of earthly vocation and made a distinction between the spiritual and the secular dimensions of God's royal power. The latter doctrine has been badly misused, especially by Lutheran theologians in Nazi Germany, but is one way of stating the insight that God's elect are in no way exempt from having their full share in the sufferings, plights, anxieties, duties, and obligations common to all men. From this perspective, full cooperation with men and women of all religions and races in the many burning issues of society and international affairs should cause no problem whatsoever. But Lutherans may be reluctant to consent to a trend that would make what is specific to Christianity, or to Judaism, disintegrate into some sectarian varieties of what is basically a common secular religion, say, an American religion of rightist or leftist brand.

The church cannot cease to believe in the gospel of God's grace in Jesus Christ, the great treasure entrusted to her and destined for all mankind. But the church should not forget that the nation to which Jesus belonged is still included in the mystery of God's election. What separates and binds together is still with us, even in the modern world.

4.

Election and the People of God

SEYMOUR SIEGEL

"From olden times," wrote Philostratus in the third century, "the Jews have been opposed not only to Rome but to the rest of humanity." The self-understanding of the Jew and his relationship to God has been a source of irritation to Jews as well as non-Jews. In a bitter pun, the rabbis pointed out that the word Sinai and *sinah* ("hatred") are related. With Sinai came hatred of the Jew.

Not only the ancient Jew and non-Jew, but their modern counterparts as well are struggling with this self-understanding. While the problem of identity has recently entered into the lexicon of sociologists and psychologists, to the Jew it has presented a perennial problem.

We will attempt briefly to schematize the filament of theological concept and living reality with which the self-understanding of the Jew is inextricably webbed.

The Biblical Picture

The whole of the biblical story involves the attempt of the creator to realize his purposes on earth. He has chosen in his mysterious way to use man as his instrument. At first, the experiment is centered on the first pair, Adam and Eve. The experiment fails. The earth is full of sinful men. The divine purpose is then directed through one family amongst the families of men, the sons of Noah. They are the only ones to survive the flood and to begin again the population of the earth. But they too sin. The divine experiment is then directed to another family, the sons of Abraham, Isaac, and Jacob.

This family is not like all other families. It is characterized by the fact that God is with its members. The meaning of this assertion is conveyed in the exegesis of the third chapter of Exodus.[1] The appellation of God, *ehyeh asher ehyeh* has been the subject of an enormous litera-

1. Cf. J. C. Murray, *The Problem of God* (New Haven: Yale University Press, 1964), and Martin Buber, *Moses: The Revelation and The Covenant* (New York: Harper & Row, 1958).

ture. But, it is established that at least one of the meanings is that God promises he will be with the people. A later echo of this is found in the Book of Isaiah (52:6), "Therefore my people shall know my name; therefore in that day they shall know that it is I who speak; here am I." The Lord will "come down" to save his people from their bondage in Egypt. The faithful presence of God among the people is the "banner" of Israel, the rallying standard about which the tribes "realize their religious and national unity as a people."[2] The most agonizing question the ancient Israelite could ask was this: "Is the Lord in our midst or not?" (Exod. 17:7). The presence of God with the people gives it its character, determines its destiny, and guarantees its future. There are some souls who doubt the persistence of God's being with them. But prophets continually assure Israel that the promise is still effective.

The biblical ideal is *shalom*. "The word is usually rendered by peace. Its fundamental meaning is totality; it means the untrammeled, free growth of the soul. But this, in its turn, means the same as harmonious community; the soul can only expand in conjunction with other souls."[3] The covenant which is a confirmation of the spirit of God amongst the people is also a guarantee of *shalom*. The words *berith* ("covenant") and *shalom* are used in conjunction with each other (Ezek. 34:25; 37:26). The two words are used interchangeably.[4] To enter the covenant is to make peace; since there is no more important covenant than the one between the people and God, there is no peace as great as that peace brought about by the harmonious living together of God and his people.

The key term in the biblical picture of the people of God is, of course, the term *berith*. "Biblical history is based on one central idea which permeates it from beginning to end; the portion of the Lord is his people; Jacob the lot of his inheritance."[5] The covenant is the hinge upon which the whole of the biblical conception turns. The being-with of God is reciprocated by the being-for of Israel. They will be my people and I will be their God. Walter Eichrodt has chosen *berith* as his central idea in the explication of the theology of the Old Testament.[6] He points out that the doctrine of *berith* involves several subconcepts which are of great importance:[7]

2. Murray, *The Problem of God*, p. 11.
3. Johannes Pedersen, *Israel* (London: Oxford University Press, 1926), 1:264.
4. Gen. 26:28; 1 Kings 5:26; Ps. 55:21; Cf. Pedersen, *Israel*, p. 285.
5. Shimon Bernfeld, *Mabo Likithbe Hakodesh* (Tel Aviv), 2:133.
6. From *Theology of the Old Testament,* vol. 1, by Walther Eichrodt. Translated by J. A. Baker. Published in the U.S.A. by The Westminster Press, 1961. Copyright © 1961, S.C.M. Press, Ltd. Used by permission.
7. *Ibid.*, pp. 37 ff.

1) The doctrine of covenant points to the "factual nature of the divine revelation." God's existence and character are not grasped through speculation or mystical contemplation. His existence and will are disclosed through the acts of history. The mighty acts of the Lord in bringing the people out of Egypt and bringing them to Mount Sinai and then to the promised land are the confirmations of the theology of the biblical man. That is why his theology is one of "recital."[8] All history is seen as leading up to the moment of covenant and all subsequent history is interpreted in its light.

2) A divine will becomes discernible which can be depended on. The great anxiety of ancient man was centered in the capriciousness of his god. He had no guarantee or assurance of the goodness of the forces who controlled his destiny. But the covenant and its adumbration gave an atmosphere of trust and security to Israelite life. They had a divine promise upon which to rely—a promise issuing forth from a being who was free yet gracious, whose *hesed* ("covenant loyalty") was forever. This led to an affirmation of life and an air of confident existence.

3) The covenant gives the human partner a unique position in the history of the world. The tribes are no longer united merely by common blood and heritage. They are united by a common obligation under the covenant. This makes it possible, also, to absorb new members into the people of God. This was an unprecedented approach in the ancient Near East. Since the people is the people of the covenant, anyone who accepted the covenant could become a member of the group. "The decisive requirement for admission is not natural kinship but readiness to submit oneself to the will of the divine Lord of the Covenant and to vow oneself to this particular God."[9]

4) The concept of *berith* leads to a "remarkably interior attitude to history." The fact that history is the matrix of the divine-human encounter gives events a crucial character. It is not nature to which a believer must conform, but the will of the living God who acts in nature and history.

5) Since the covenant is the central concept, purely national interests, though important, are not absolute. If the national institutions assisted in the observance of the obligations of the *berith* they were the recipients of the divine grace and solicitude. If they frustrated the divine purpose then they, too, could be destroyed.

8. Cf. G. E. Wright, *The God Who Acts* (London: S.C.M. Press, 1952).
9. Eichrodt, *Theology of the Old Testament*, p. 39.

Covenant and Law

The acting out of the covenant is expressed on the level of the law of the Torah. (Law, of course, is not an appropriate translation of Torah.) The covenant is sustained and concretized through the Torah. The Torah is a sign of God's grace to Israel, for it makes it possible for the people to relate itself to its covenant partner. The observance of the Torah is part of the knowledge of God (*da-at elohim*). When the *da-at elohim* is missing there is a breaking of the law and horrible immorality (Hosea). The relationship between covenant law and grace is expressed in the liturgy of the synagogue:

> With everlasting love hast Thou loved the house of Israel
> Thou hast revealed to us a law and commandments, statutes and judgments . . .
> They are our life and the measure of our days.[10]

Through the observance of the law, there are brought forth *otot*, signs and remembrances of the covenant. Just as in the ancient Near East when treaties were set up between human partners there were certain monuments or other clear signs, so Israel through its law testifies to the covenant. The two most important *otot* are the Sabbath and circumcision. The Sabbath is the sign of the covenant between God and nature and the circumcision is the sign of the covenant of the people. The *ot* is sealed into the flesh of every male, and in the organ of generation, thus to testify to the eternal nature of the covenant which is transmitted from one generation to the other. The law also serves as a reminder of the covenant and of the events which formed the character of the people, especially the going out of Egypt. Thus the festivals and other observances are signs and reinforcements of the *berith*. The *berith* without the law is an idea without an expression.

Covenant and the Land

The covenant promises always involve the land of promise. Thus, the confession of faith which is found in the twenty-fourth chapter of Joshua consists of a recital of the great deeds of the Lord with his people and an acceptance on the part of the people of the obligations of the cove-

10. *The Authorized Daily Prayer Book of the United Hebrew Congregation of the British Empire*, new translation by S. Singer (London: Eyre Spottiswoodie, 1915), p. 39.

nant. Part of the whole event is the reiteration of the promise of the land. Professor Abraham J. Heschel in his recent volume *Israel*, has written: "There is a unique association between the people and the land of Israel. Even before Israel becomes a people, the land is preordained for Israel. . . . Even before there was a people, there was a promise. The promise of a land. The election of Abraham and the election of the land came together. The promise of the land to the patriarchs is the leitmotif in the Five Books of Moses. . . . Beyond the promise of the land and increasing posterity, the promise to Abraham was a blessing for all the families of the earth. The gift of the land is an earnest of a greater promise."[11] This is an important consideration in understanding the biblical conception of chosenness and covenant. The choosing and the holiness involved in it is concrete, everyday, and not limited to cult and dogma. In the Bible, and in Judaism, there is no bifurcation of the secular and the religious, of the concrete and the spiritual. "Body and soul are like friends and lovers to each other."[12] The identification of the real with the heavenly and the unreal with the worldly is foreign to the Bible, and to Judaism. The Bible is not allegory nor is it to be spiritualized. It is tied to earth, land, life, and conflict. Thus there is a covenant with the people, with the land, and with the future. The Hebrew Bible is not a book about heaven. It is a book about the earth. The word *erets* ("land") occurs at least five times as often in the Bible as the word *shamayim* ("heaven").[13]

Kiddush Hashem (The Sanctification of the Name)

Kiddush hashem becomes the supreme responsibility of those who live under the covenant. *Kiddush hashem* means "to bear witness to the God of Israel, amidst the idolatries of the world, to proclaim in word and deed, in life and thought, that there is no real God but the Transcendent One and to 'give the world no rest until it acknowledges the sovereignty of the Lord.' "[14] Through the performance of good deeds on the part of the people of God, the name of God is sanctified amongst the nations of the world. The ultimate test of *kiddush hashem* is martyrdom, testifying with the whole of one's being to the faith which gives life. The obverse

11. Abraham J. Heschel, *Israel: An Echo of Eternity* (New York: Farrar, Straus & Giroux, 1970), p. 100.
12. *Midrash Ha neelam*, Zohar, vol. 1, 134b, quoted by Heschel, *Israel*, p. 145.
13. Heschel, *Israel*, p. 103.
14. Will Herberg, "The Chosenness of Israel and the Jews of Today," *Midstream* 1 (Autumn 1955): 83–91.

of *kiddush hashem* is *chillul hashem*, desecration of the name, acting in such a way that the cause of God is diminished among men. This responsibility puts a fearsome burden upon the people of God. They are not always equal to the task, but they do not have the option to abandon it. This idea of *kiddush hashem* reaches its apex in the prophetic idea of the suffering servant. Though there are many interpretations of this concept, it is clear that the prophetic assertion is that Israel is the suffering servant, who, because it is God's people, has frequently to bear suffering and pain. When the world is not ready to accept the yoke of ethical behavior, it tragically turns upon those who represent the divine demand.

The being-with of God with the people is not always pleasant. When the people of Israel sin, they are not only doing the wrong thing, but they are blaspheming against the Holy One of Israel and are therefore subject to punishment. God's wrath is kindled against them (Deut. 29:19). But God is also true to his covenant. He will not forsake his people even when they sin. Because God has a special relationship with his people, he visits upon them all their iniquities (Amos 3:2).

Being God's people implies a delicate balance. The Jew is of the world. The Jew, in fact, is charged with sanctifying the world and all that is in it, with making holiness live, justice breathe, wisdom mature, joy perdure. He is in the world and through the world his chosenness is expressed. Yet, he must not, under pain of disobeying the partner in the covenant, be so attached to the world that he is overcome by it and puts his trust in men or horses. This is the entrance gate of the most horrible of crimes and sins in Jewish thought, idolatry.

The Rabbinic Elaboration

The basic biblical picture is further elaborated by the rabbis. "There is not a single endearing epithet in the language such as brother, sister, bride, mother, lamb, or eye which is not, according to the rabbis, applied by Scripture to express the intimate relation between God and His people."[15] It is the task of Israel to declare the unity of God by proclaiming the *shema*, and likewise the Holy Spirit proclaims the election of Israel by saying: Who is like thy people Israel?[16] When the people of Israel suffer, so does God suffer with them.[17] The subjection of Israel implies God's subjection and the presence accompanies the Israelites through their

15. Solomon Schechter, *Aspects of Rabbinic Theology* (New York: Schocken Books, 1961), p. 46.
16. *Mekilta,* ed. Meier Friedmann (Vienna, 1870), 36b.
17. *Seder Eliyahu Rabba,* ed. Meier Friedmann (Vienna, 1900), p. 89.

sufferings. Therefore, when Israel will be redeemed, God himself, so to speak, will be redeemed.

The rabbinic period saw the creation of the liturgy and thus the belief in the election of Israel finds its clearest expression in what the synagogue prayed as well as preached: "Thou hast chosen us from all peoples; thou hast loved us and taken pleasure in us, and hast exalted us above all tongues; thou hast sanctified us by thy commandments and brought us near unto Thy service; O our King, thou hast called us by thy great and holy name."[18]

The relationship between Israel and the Creator is so close that it was predestined before the creation of the world and existed before the world itself (Genesis Rabba 1:4). Schechter quotes a very remarkable rabbinic statement: "The matter is to be compared to a king who was desiring to build; but when he was digging for the purpose of laying the foundations, he found only swamps and mire. At last he hit on a rock, when he said, 'Here will I build.' So, too, when God was about to create the world, he foresaw the sinful generations of Enosh (when man began to profane the name of the Lord), and the wicked generations of the deluge (which said unto God, Depart from us), and he said, 'How shall I create the world whilst these generations are certain to provoke me (by their crimes and sin)?' But, when he perceived that Abraham would one day arise, he said, 'Behold I have found the *petra* on which to build and base the world.' " The patriarch Abraham is called the rock (Isa. 51:1–2); and so the people of Israel are called the rocks (Num. 33:9).[19] The most common explanation for the singling out of Israel is the legend which relates that the Torah was offered to all the nations. They refused it, each for his own particular reason, until Israel said: we will do and will obey.

But, for all of this celebration of the importance of Israel, there is no exclusivism. It was the Israelites in the talmudic period who taught the principle of the seven Noachian commandments by means of which the righteous of all the world have a share in the world to come. There is a kind of general revelation which is the common heritage of all mankind. The observance of these commandments is the duty of everyone. The children of Israel living under a special covenant have additional responsibilities. But both Jew and gentile have a share in redemption.[20]

18. *The Authorized Daily Prayer Book*, p. 227.
19. *Yalamdenu* in *Yalut*, Number 766, quoted by Schechter in *Aspects of Rabbinic Theology*, p. 59.
20. See the literature cited by Louis Finkelstein in *The Pharisees: Sociological Background of Their Faith* (Philadelphia: Jewish Publication Society of America, 1962), 2: p. 881, n. 22.

The turning point in the rabbinic period occurred in the year 70 C.E. ("Common Era") when the temple and the commonwealth were destroyed. The disaster of 70 was compounded by the ill-fated rebellion of 135 C.E. under Bar Kokba. The special relationship of Israel and God could not but be called into question. There is even a semihumorous story recorded in the Talmud: "R. Joshua b. Hananiah was standing in the house of Caesar. A certain Min showed (in pantomime) a people from whom whose God had turned his face. He (R. Joshua) showed him (in pantomime) His hand stretched out over us. Caesar said to R. Joshua what did he show you? A people whose Lord hath turned away His face from them, and I showed him His hand is stretched out over us." As great as the catastrophe must have seemed, the rabbis assured the people that God was still with them. Indeed, he himself, so to speak, was suffering with them. The sufferings were seen as a testing of the people rather than a rejection. "Flax," they said "improves when threshed, but only when it is of good quality . . . a potter does not tap to test a cracked vessel, lest it break. He tests only the perfect vessel. God tries the righteous" (Hagiga 5b). Of course, there was now increased stress on the eschatological justification of Israel. The sufferings of the righteous would cease when the Messiah came. It was now the duty of the righteous to speed the redemption through their good deeds and study. The people were to prepare the way for the eventual kingdom (or kingship) of God.

The Challenge of Christianity

The most serious challenge to Judaism in ancient times was the new community of Christianity. Justin Martyr says: "Those who follow Christ are the true Israel; the children of the promise; they are the true successors of those Jews who found justification in times past."[21]

The assertion of the new Christian community was that although the idea of chosenness is central to the Bible, and although the descendants of Abraham, Isaac, and Jacob had indeed been chosen once, now the covenant had been abrogated and a new one concluded with the true believers in Jesus. The law had been superseded and a new Israel created. The old Israel was at best a reminder of the old promises. Judaism was an anachronism, the Jew a stubborn fellow who refused to see the truth. The Gospels were apparently reedited to express hostility to the Jews.

21. Quoted by Hans Joachim Schoeps in *The Jewish-Christian Argument: A History of Theologies in Conflict* (New York: Holt, Rinehart & Winston, 1963), p. 29.

The reaction of the rabbis to this claim was not direct. Even to argue the point was demeaning to a Jew, for it made the whole history of Jewish martyrdom and witnessing a cruel joke. The great Jewish historian Graetz observed that although the Mishna devotes a special tractate to the laws concerning heathen, there are no laws regarding Christians,[22] and the Mishna does not in any place touch directly on the subject of Christianity. The rabbis emphasize repeatedly that the purpose and end of the election of the people of Israel was to observe the Torah which was a sign of his grace.

As has frequently been pointed out, Judaism does not see Christianity as a real theological problem. But Judaism does present an agonizing problem to Christianity for, if the Jewish claim is true, then Christianity is called into question. Yet, in the medieval period, especially, Christianity and Islam were seen as fulfilling a providential plan. Maimonides sees the two daughter faiths as serving in part the fulfillment of Israel's vocation. "The ways of God are beyond our wisdom to comprehend," he writes, "but he seems to be using the two faiths to perfect the entire world to serve him," thus, (thanks to the efforts of Christianity and Islam) "the entire world has been enlightened with the teachings concerning the Messiah, the Torah, and the commandments; and these teachings have been disseminated to distant lands among many peoples."[23]

The story of the relationship between Judaism and Christianity is a painful one. The solution to the tension between the two faiths can be found, it seems to me, only through a recognition by Christianity that whatever are the truths of that faith it cannot claim to supersede Judaism. A helpful approach is suggested by the great German-Jewish theologian, Franz Rosenzweig: "Our recognition of Christianity rests, in fact, upon Christianity, namely, upon the fact that Christianity recognizes us. It is the Torah, ultimately, which is spread abroad by Bible societies to the most distant lands. . . . No one comes to the Father—except through him (that is Jesus). No one comes . . . but the situation is different when one need no longer come to the Father because he is already with him. That is the case of the nation of Israel."[24]

Rosenzweig is saying that there may very well be a new covenant or testament in addition to the old one. But this new one, Christianity, does not abrogate the old one; its function is instead to make it possible for

22. Heinrich Graetz, *Divrei Yeme Yisrael* (Warsaw, 1893–1916), 2: 315 ff.

23. *Mishne Torah, Hilchot Melakhim*, chap. 11.

24. Quoted in Schoeps, *The Jewish-Christian Argument*, p. 141.

the nations of the world to enter into the Israelite covenant. Christianity, in Rosenzweig's view, is the Judaism of the gentiles.

Challenges: Modern Times (With Reference to Ancient and Modern Pagans)

The challenge to the self-understanding of the Jews as being the people of God predates the beginning of Christianity. As early as about 300 B.C.E. Hecateus of Abdera, a Greek living in Egypt, asserted that the Jews were cast out of Egypt because they were lepers and criminals. The Greeks and Romans saw in Judaism a misanthropic religion feeding the need to exalt oneself by demeaning others.

But this approach is not limited to ancient times: "Question [put to G. B. Shaw]: What do you think about the racist theories of the Nazis? Answer: This is a silly scientific theory. But what arouses amazement is the fact that the anti-semites do not realize how Jewish their outlook is. The Jew's problem is his great arrogance, which is based on his faith that he belongs to a god-chosen people. The absurdity of the Nordics is just an attempt to imitate the grandchildren of Abraham."[25] These sentiments have recently been echoed by Toynbee who accuses Judaism of introducing intolerance and self-centeredness into the world. In Toynbee's view, the Bible and the religions based upon it are infected with a fanaticism which threatens to destroy the fabric of humanity.[26] The reply to these assertions, of course, is that the authentic notion of chosenness does not imply the right of sovereignty. To compare the mad Nazi idea with the biblical assertion is like comparing a monkey with a human being.

As in so many other instances, Benedict Spinoza is the spokesman for the new turn in thinking which is characteristic of modern times. Spinoza, who saw the past as a long series of enslaving superstitions, sought to free mankind from what he thought were the ideas which were blocking progress. In his *Tractatus Theologico-Politicus* he devotes a chapter to the vocation of the Hebrews. He concludes that the doctrine of election is to be understood as the adoption by any group of a certain way of life: "We can now easily understand what is meant by the election of God. For since no one can do anything save by the predetermined order of nature, that is by God's eternal ordinance and decree, it follows that no one can choose a plan of life for himself or accomplish any work save

25. Quoted in Herberg, "The Chosenness of Israel," p. 89.
26. *New York Times,* 3 February 1969.

by God's vocation choosing him for the work or the plan of life in question, rather than any other."[27] Spinoza concludes that since the Jewish commonwealth has disappeared and there is no specifically Jewish way, now, of political organization, the election of Israel has ceased. The fact of Jewish survival is explained by the persistence of gentile hatred of Jews and also by the rite of circumcision which has served to keep the Jews apart. However, there is no reason for the Jews to remain separate anymore; their chosenness has been dissolved and only the hatred of others and the spite of their leaders keep the Jews in existence. In a strangely prophetic passage, Spinoza concludes his chapter with the words: "Nay, I would go so far as to say that if the foundations of their religion have not emasculated their minds that they may even, if occasion offers, so changeable are human affairs, raise up their empire afresh, and that God may a second time elect them."[28]

Liberals and radicals of all stripes, including Jews, have assailed the idea of chosenness as being anachronistic and even pernicious. Recently, there appeared a collection of essays by the well-known Marxist historian, Isaac Deutscher.[29] He sees as a contradiction the idea of a universal God and the idea of a chosen people. He hails Spinoza for first discovering this "cardinal contradiction in Judaism." In surveying the lives of Heine, Marx, Rosa Luxembourg, Trotsky, and Freud, Deutscher salutes them as true revolutionaries who tried to break down the barriers between men. "All of these went beyond the boundaries of Jewry. They all found Jewry too narrow, too archaic, and too constricting." It was this effort to transcend nationalities, religions, and cultures that made them great. The assertion of Deutscher and others like him is that by transcending Jewishness the genius can rise above his "times and generations, and strike out mentally into wide new horizons and far into the future."[30]

The falseness of this assertion is apparent when one understands that it is impossible to achieve unless one has roots. The ultimate irony is that a person like Trotsky who was so adamant against claims to sustain Jewishness was to experience the following: "Nearly a quarter of a century later, while he was engaged in an unequal struggle with Stalin and went to the party cells in Moscow to expound his views, he was met with

27. Benedict Spinoza, *Tractatus*, unabridged Elwes translation (London: G. Bell & Sons, 1900–1901), p. 45.

28. *Ibid.*, p. 56.

29. Isaac Deutscher, *The Non-Jewish Jew* (London and New York: Oxford University Press, 1968).

30. *Ibid.*, p. 27.

vicious allusions to his Jewishness and even with plain anti-semitic insults."[31] The universal man, ex-Jew, is always confronted with his own Jewishness. The ancient election, even in its twisted form, pursues him like Nemesis.

Challenges—Theological

The serious challenge to the consciousness of the Jews as the "people of God" comes from two quarters: one, from the theological reconstruction called for by Professor Mordecai Kaplan and from those who have rejected the idea of chosenness because of Auschwitz.

Professor Mordecai Kaplan has towered above the American Jewish scene as its guide, critic, and innovator. His idea of God is naturalistic. God is defined as those processes and relations within life which make life abundant and contribute to salvation. God is not to be conceived as a person, but rather as a process or perhaps the sum of the processes in the cosmos which assist human beings in realizing themselves. As a result of his call for a thorough reconstruction of Judaism, Kaplan has consistently opposed the idea of the chosen people. He has called it a divisive and even an arrogant idea. He has called for its removal from Jewish teaching and has amended the liturgy to eliminate reference to the notion of chosenness.

But, even Professor Kaplan insists that the Jewish people has a special task or vocation to perform, that is, to show how nationalism and religion might be combined. Though he eschews the idea of chosenness, he cannot deny that Israel is in some way the "people of God."

The most poignant challenge to the doctrine of Israel's uniqueness in our times comes from the experience of the Holocaust. How can we expect to believe in God and in the God of the covenant when such unspeakable acts were committed without any intervention by a supposedly benign God? Can anyone believe in the special relationship of Israel and the Almighty when a million Jewish children went to their deaths?

If chosenness demands sacrifice and martyrdom, perhaps we should abandon it. Let us be like the other nations. A gifted Yiddish poetess of our time, Kadya Maladowska, has expressed the yearning to slough off the yoke of hatred visited upon the Jew because of his chosenness:

31. *Ibid.*, p. 37.

Merciful God, choose another people
We are weary from dying
We have no more prayers
Choose another people
We have no more blood
To shed as a sacrifice
Merciful God
Give us ordinary clothes
Of shepherds of flocks
Of smiths who stand by the anvil
Of clothes-washers, or tanners
And do us one more kindness
Merciful God
Take away your *schechina* [holy presence] from us.[32]

However, it is the experience of the Holocaust which seems to have confirmed, perhaps in a perverse way, the uniqueness of Israel. The very fury and irrationalism of the persecution seems to confirm that the Jew stands for something which tyrants cannot abide. Professor Emil Fackenheim has expressed this in a very moving way: "Most assuredly no redeeming Voice is heard from Auschwitz, or ever will be heard. However, a commanding voice is being heard and has, however faintly, been heard from the start. Religious Jews hear it and they identify its source. Secularist Jews also hear it, even though perforce they leave it unidentified. At Auschwitz Jews came face to face with absolute evil. They were and still are singled out by it, but in the midst of it they hear an absolute commandment: Jews are forbidden to grant posthumous victories to Hitler. They are commanded to survive as Jews, lest the Jewish people perish."[33]

The very determination to persist and survive, even if secularly motivated, is an expression of the Jewish attachment to a divine command. The overwhelming response of Jews all over the world to the threat to the state of Israel in June, 1967, is testimony that this determination lies dormant in the vast majority of Jewish souls around the world.

An important element of this consciousness is the attachment which Jews feel to the state of Israel. This does not only reflect the triumph of the Jewish people, rising from the ashes to re-create itself. It also is a reconfirmation of the Jewish desire to express Jewishness not only under conditions of exile, but also in a situation of independence. The land and

32. [Translated by S. S.]
33. Emil Fackenheim, "Jewish Faith and the Holocaust," *Commentary* 46 (August 1968): 30–36.

the promise have always gone hand in hand. A threat to the Jewish community in the land of Israel was perceived not only as a political act but as a threat to the very existence of the covenant and all it implies. As Heschel put it: "We felt all of Jewish history present in a moment."[34] Many felt that they were part of a "mysterious movement of Jewish history." The biblical commandment and the biblical promise were tied to the land and no Jew was able to withstand the call that came to him in the crucial days of 1967.

It cannot be stressed too often that Judaism and Jewishness are not to be seen as spiritualized. Jerusalem is the real place, not a heavenly city; the holy land is the holy land, not a spiritual fellowship, and the people is a real people, not a creedal fellowship. Jews, of course, share enthusiastically the political life of the countries in which they live. But because the Bible is active in their lives, the consciousness of the importance of the land of promise cannot be completely suppressed.

More Confirmations

The unique character of the children of Abraham, Isaac, and Jacob has received confirmation from hitherto unlooked for sources. Roger Shinn has pointed out that totalitarians find the Jews a reminder by their very existence of a universalism they cannot tolerate. It is not what the Jew happens to believe that is resented and persecuted. These things happen to him because of his very existence as a Jew. Totalitarians with their total claim upon the individual feel threatened by one who stands for allegiance to the universal God. (The same, of course, is true of Christians; but Jews are hated because they are Jews; Christians because they are *believing* Christians.)

Professor Will Herberg has described the feeling of uniqueness, of special obligation, which permeates the consciousness of most Jews even when they vociferously repudiate any kind of theological doctrine of chosenness. The feeling that something special is expected of him, that some burden has been placed upon him (witness the perverse way this is affirmed by Philip Roth in *Portnoy's Complaint*) is testimony to the survival of the ancient covenant idea. "I have yet to find a Jew," writes Herberg, "who does not in some manner of form exhibit this profound sense of 'difference' and special vocation."[35]

34. Heschel, *Israel*, p. 198.
35. Herberg, "The Chosenness of Israel," p. 89.

It is this persistence which explains the fury of anti-Semitism now raising its ugly head again all over the world. However it may express itself, at bottom anti-Semitism and anti-Judaism reflect the revolt of man and society against the God of the Bible and his demands. "Hatred of Judaism is at bottom hatred of Christianity" (Maritain).[36] For, as Franz Rosenzweig observed: "Whenever the pagan within the Christian soul rises in revolt against the yoke of the Cross, he vents his fury on the Jew."[37]

The People of God Perdures

The traditional doctrine persists even today. It affirms that the Jewish people is not an ordinary people like all peoples, but one called into being by God to serve his purposes in the world. The choosing is a vocation, a summons, and a sending. It is an obligation to stand witness amidst the idolatries of the world to the power, justice, and love of the everliving God. To bear this uniqueness has not been easy. By not fitting into any known scheme, Israel "thwarts the nation's very natural desire for an explanation. . . . The existence of whatever cannot be cubbyholed and hence understood is alarming . . . the Jewish people was, indeed, always a 'sinister, homeless spectre.' "[38]

Jews know they are a living community, not "spectres," a community rooted in the world yet transcending it. Jews are part of the nations of the world as loyal citizens, but are also tied to the land of promise not because they are covetous, but, as Buber put it in his letter to Mahatma Gandhi: "Our one desire is that at last we may be able to obey."[39]

Nothing is as telling as the words put on the lips of Ernie, the hero of Andre Schwartz-Bart's novel, *The Last of the Just.* Together with a group of children and his own wife he is led to the gas chamber. He prays wearily and believingly, "O God, O Lord, we went forward like this thousands of years ago. We walked across arid deserts and blood red seas, through floods of salt-bitter tears. We are very old, we are still walking. Oh let us arrive finally."[40]

Consciousness of uniqueness; persistence of belief; eternal hope.

36. *Ibid.*

37. *Ibid.*

38. Reprinted by permission of Schocken Books Inc. from *Israel and the World* by Martin Buber. Copyright © 1948, 1963 by Schocken Books Inc., pp. 167–68.

39. *Ibid.*, p. 230.

40. Andre Schwartz-Bart, *The Last of the Just* (New York: Atheneum, 1960), p. 374.

PART TWO

LAND—PEOPLE—STATE

5.

The Promise and the Land

RONALD M. HALS

In this paper I shall attempt to provide a basis for discussion of the theme of "the promise and the land" by surveying the use which this idea has received in the biblical literature which is our heritage. Because Lutherans affirm the biblical heritage to be authoritative, such a survey is the only possible foundation for an examination of this theme "from a Lutheran perspective."[1] I shall try to conduct this survey of past usage in such a way that its implications for possible present treatments of the same theme will be evident.

The Subject in the Old Testament[2]

The idea of the promise of a land occurs about twenty times in the Tetrateuch, usually in combination with the promise of descendants, blessing, and/or a new relationship to God. In addition, thirteen times in Deuteronomy the idea of the promise of a land occurs, and there it is always the land alone which is the subject of the promise. In later literature beyond the Pentateuch additional references are made to this same subject of the promise and the land, but these will be taken up later on. Compared to some other Old Testament themes, this one is not too difficult to get ahold of. While the idea of a word study does not commend itself, for the term "land" (*erets*) is too broad a one, meaning "earth" as well, this does not pose a serious problem. Regardless of terminology, the passages dealing with the promise of a land are readily

1. The description of this paper's task was suggested by the Division of Theological Studies of the Lutheran Council in the U.S.A.

2. Because of the nontechnical purpose of this occasion, and because a description of widely held views rather than any personal idiosyncracies of my own is called for, what I shall present here is a summary of that article which I feel best reflects the consensus of Christian Old Testament scholarship on this subject, "The Promised Land and Yahweh's Land in the Hexateuch," by Gerhard von Rad. The article can be found in his *The Problem of the Hexateuch and Other Essays* (Edinburgh, London: Oliver & Boyd, 1966), pp. 79–93.

recognizable and relatively straightforward. The only additional term used to any extent to designate this land involved in the promise is that of "inheritance" (*nachalah*).

The passages in question are also relatively clear when it comes to form. Their form is that of a promise, that is, an announcement of a future gift. The passages occur in the first person, in which God himself offers this promise; examples are also found in which the promise is discussed by others, so that God is portrayed as speaking in the third person. A large number of the instances involve the use of a special form of promise, the oath. The primary intent of this use of the oath form seems to be simply the underlining of the certainty of the promise given.

The first surprise to be encountered in the survey of the subject of the promise and the land occurs when we attempt to examine the history of the idea. In the old summaries which seem to lie behind the present structure of the Hexateuch, such as Deut. 26:5–10, no reference is made to our theme. Since the idea is prominent in all three of the major Pentateuchal sources, J, E, and P, it would seem to have been inserted into the structure of the creedal summaries by the Yahwist, the oldest of these three narrators. Recently scholars have tended to answer with rather a high degree of unanimity the question of whence the Yahwist derived this idea. The answer given is that the promise of the land was an element of pre-Mosaic patriarchal religion, being a part of the worship of the "God of the fathers."[3] The original significance of the content of such a promise also seems reasonably obvious. What else could be involved other than a promise to the patriarchs living on the edge of a settled land that they shall one day have it for their own possession (cf. Gen. 15:7 f.)? However, a quick examination of the use of the promise of the land in the present book of Genesis makes it plain that this is no longer how the matter is understood. In his portrayal of the theme of the promise and the land the Yahwist has subjected the idea to considerable revision. Now the promise is tied to a fulfillment which takes place under Joshua, not one which took place in the lifetime of the original patriarchs as the simple promise itself would have seemed to indicate. The Yahwist has even introduced the theme of the promise of the land into sagas where it had originally no place at all (cf. Gen. 28:13). It is important that what is being said here should be clearly

3. Albrecht Alt, "The God of the Fathers," *Essays on Old Testament History and Religion* (Oxford: Blackwell, 1966), pp. 3–77.

understood. The point is that the original promise of the land envisaged no second entry. That is, Abraham, Isaac, and Jacob are promised the land in such a way that it seems clear that they themselves are to receive the possession of this land and then pass it on to their descendants. Any idea of a lengthy delay in the fulfillment of this promise, so that it will only be their later descendants in the days of Joshua who will receive the land to possess, seems not at all to be suggested in the wording of the original promise. This revision by the Yahwist of the significance of the promise is, of course, associated with the present structure of the Hexateuch. However, it creates a somewhat different perspective for an understanding of the relationship of the patriarchs to the promise of the land, since the fulfillment is now so much delayed. It gives the patriarchs a rather dialectical relationship to the land. That is, they are portrayed as having been granted the land but not yet possessing it. The word used to describe their relationship to the land is that of "sojourning." A further aspect of the Yahwist's revision of the promise of the land is to extend it to apply to the greater Israel, not just to the patriarchal family. The way in which this greater Israel came to be and the complications involved in the exodus and entry into the land are here passed over.

When we look more closely at the particular way in which the Yahwist himself introduces the promise of the land, we see how in Gen. 12:1–3 the land is omitted from the content of the promise as first given to Abraham. It seems that this reflects the intent of the Yahwist to present the original promise in Gen. 12:1–3 as a test of Abraham's blind obedience. Then, after he meets this test by leaving his ancestral land, the actual promise of the land is added in verse 7 of chapter 12. By this means the promise of the land actually gains in import. But, at the same time, the focus of the narrative clearly but subtly shifts to that of the secondary experience, that is, the experience of those descendants of Abraham who look back and see the characteristic of God's dealing with them in the light of his dealing with their ancestor Abraham. This blending of the primary experience with the secondary experience is one which is characteristic of the saga form and also the apparent result of conscious effort by the Yahwist, who seeks to make this history significant in his present situation for an audience at a later time.[4]

There are, however, other Hexateuchal approaches to the theme of the promise and the land. The one which deserves our attention for a

4. The terminology is that used by Gerhard von Rad in *Genesis* (Philadelphia: Westminster, 1961), pp. 3–42.

time is the one to which we are introduced by the phrase in Lev. 25:23, "The land is mine; you are only sojourners." This is manifestly a different tradition. According to the Yahwist, the land belonged to the nations and was never said to be God's land. The idea that the land belonged to God is indeed an old and basic one, especially in the cultic sphere. The idea of the sabbatical year has its roots here, as do also the ideas of tithes and first fruits. According to the imagery suggested by this view, portions of land were allotted to individuals as their "inheritance." The details as to the precise way in which such allotment took place, whether only in some original type of large scale division of the land or more likely in a periodic reassignment, are not fully known to us. The term "inheritance" in the Hexateuch refers primarily to the portion belonging to a certain tribe, but of course an individual within a tribe also has an inheritance, as becomes clear in many other passages, such as the one about Naboth's vineyard. Incidentally, Josh. 22:19 implies that it is really only the land west of the Jordan which is Yahweh's land, whereas the relationship to Yahweh of the land east of the Jordan is debatable. This same point of view is reflected in the proposed reconstruction described in Ezek. 48.

In summary, it appears that this last notion of the inheritance is a cultic one, while the view of the promised land is a "historical" one. The Hexateuchal narrative is governed by the historical outlook, but the Hexateuchal legislation is dominated by the cultic conception, even down to the latest laws such as those concerning the jubilee year. In the account of the division of the land these conceptions are combined. Here apparently Deuteronomistic and priestly perspectives are involved.

To give a somewhat brief look at the nature of the way Deuteronomy and the priestly materials treat our theme, the following quick summary is offered. The priestly writer sees the patriarchs as only sojourners, but still as ones who do get an "earnest" of the fulfillment of this promise through their acquisition of a burial place. Deuteronomy, in line with its hortatory orientation, sees obedience to the commandments as the condition for the reception and possession of the land. However, Deuteronomy also expands the concept of "inheritance" to apply to all Israel. The land is Israel's inheritance. But, of course, Deuteronomy dates from after the time of the settlement, and this viewpoint can only be a kind of fiction. Still, more than fiction is involved. Beyond fiction we have here a kind of eschatological perspective. Those promises already having been fulfilled are once again set before the assembly of all Israel as applying anew to those who decide for Yahweh in the "today" of decision. The concept "rest" receives a similar eschatological reinterpretation in Deuteronomy. The implication seems to be that a promise is not exhausted by its fulfillment, but remains as promise, although undergoing a metamorphosis to some extent. The promise of the land becomes the promise of a future benefit of God's redemptive activity.

If the question is asked whether there are other approaches to our theme beyond the bounds of the Hexateuch, the answer must be yes. We shall temporarily skip the way in which the prophets deal with this theme, but other bodies of Old Testament material also pick up the question of the promise and the land. "Picking up" is exactly what seems to be involved. A familiar theme is once again taken up and further elaborated by later generations. Two prominent examples can be cited.

The first example is what is called "Levitical" piety in the psalms.[5] In Ps. 142:5 we encounter the line, "God is my portion." Similar thoughts and terminology occur in Ps. 16:5 ff. Here we seem to be encountering the spiritualization of an old idea. According to old tradition, reflected in Num. 18:20 and Deut. 10:9, God is Levi's "portion and inheritance." Because the tribe of Levi received no allotment of land, but was set apart for service in the sanctuary, the imagery of describing Levi's portion or inheritance as being God is readily understandable. But in the psalms this kind of reference, originally of significance only for Levites, is expanded and extended so as to apply to any Israelite, hence the name "Levitical" piety. A name such as Hilkiah, meaning "my portion is Yahweh," reflects the same idea in a relatively old Yahwistic name. The significance of what it means to have Yahweh as one's portion is rather astonishing when one looks further at psalms such as 16. Psalm 16:9–11 reflects an extreme degree of spiritualization in which having God as one's portion is understood to imply an inheritance whose blessing is greater than the threat of death.

> Therefore my heart is glad, and my soul rejoices;
>   my body also dwells secure.
> For thou dost not give me up to Sheol,
>   or let thy godly one see the Pit.
> Thou dost show me the path of life;
>   in thy presence there is fullness of joy,
>   in thy right hand are pleasures for evermore.

5. von Rad, " 'Righteousness' and 'Life' in the Cultic Language of the Psalms," *The Problem of the Hexateuch and Other Essays*, pp. 260–264.

That this imagery and the use it receives in Ps. 16 are not rare and isolated elements in the Psalter is demonstrated by the way the same terminology and the same content occur again in Ps. 73:23–28.

> Nevertheless I am continually with thee;
> thou dost hold my right hand.
> Thou dost guide me with thy counsel,
> and afterward thou wilt receive me to glory.
> Whom have I in heaven but thee?
> and there is nothing upon earth that I desire besides thee.
> My flesh and my heart may fail,
> but God is the strength of my heart and my portion for ever.
>
> For lo, those who are far from thee shall perish;
> thou dost put an end to those who are false to thee.
> But for me it is good to be near God;
> I have made the Lord God my refuge,
> that I may tell of all thy works.

Once again we notice the way in which the idea of "portion" is used to describe an individual's relationship to God. And again, as in Ps. 16, this Levitical piety describes an assurance which is of sufficient power to overcome the threat of death and the meaninglessness which that threat had introduced into life, as described in the earlier verses of this same psalm.

The second instance of the use of the theme of the promise and the land outside the bounds of the Hexateuch is that of the Deuteronomistic historian. Here the theory of Martin Noth is assumed, according to which the Book of Deuteronomy is inserted as the beginning of the work of the Deuteronomistic historian.[6] Chapters 5 and 30 of Deuteronomy are basically a book of Torah which existed before the Deuteronomistic historian and to which he has supplied an introduction, namely chapters 1 to 3 or possibly 4 of Deuteronomy. However, at a few spots in this old preexisting book of Torah, the Deuteronomistic historian (henceforth referred to as Dtr) has made some revisions to update the material to suit the needs of his own exilic audience. The date of Dtr is sufficiently indicated by the fact that the last episode in his history refers to an event of 561 B.C. In Deut. 30:1 ff. Dtr seems to be applying the book of Torah to this exilic situation. He refers to that situation, "when all these things come upon you, the blessing and the curse, which I have set before you, and you call them to mind among all the nations where the

6. Martin Noth, *Überlieferungsgeschichtliche Studien* (Halle/Saale: M. Niemeyer, 1943), 1:3–110.

Lord your God has driven you, and return to the Lord your God . . ." In this exilic situation Dtr reapplies the old promise of the land. Upon Israel's repentance ("return"),

> The Lord your God will restore your fortunes, and have compassion upon you, and he will gather you again from all the peoples where the Lord your God has scattered you. If your outcasts are in the uttermost parts of heaven, from there the Lord your God will gather you, and from there he will fetch you; and the Lord your God will bring you into the land which your fathers possessed, that you may possess it; and he will make you more prosperous and numerous than your fathers.

Once again the old promise has been subjected to a reinterpretation so that it can speak again beyond its original fulfillment.

The Subject in the New Testament

For Christians the question of the further use of the theme of the promise and the land by biblical writers does not end here, for Christians go on to encounter this same type of reinterpretation of the old promise in the New Testament. In Heb. 11:8 ff. we once again encounter the theme of the promise of the land. It is observed that Abraham was called to "a place which he was to receive as an inheritance." Then, before the actual receiving of this land, "he sojourned in the land of promise, as in a foreign land, living in tents with Isaac and Jacob, heirs with him of the same promise." The use of the Hexateuchal terminology of promise, inheritance, and sojourning is obvious. But the writer of the Letter to the Hebrews is not content simply to repeat the old tradition. In verses 9 and 10 he sets up a contrast between Abraham's living in tents and his looking forward "to the city which has foundations, whose builder and maker is God." The way in which this combination of traditions is applied to the Christian audience the writer has in mind becomes clear in verse 13. There it is said of the earlier generations that "these all died in faith, not having received what was promised, but having seen it and greeted it from afar, and having acknowledged that they were strangers and exiles on the earth . . . people . . . seeking a homeland." The writer observes:

> If they had been thinking of that land from which they had gone out, they would have had opportunity to return. But as it is, they desire a better country, that is, a heavenly one. Therefore God is not ashamed to be called their God, for he has prepared for them a city.

It is of considerable interest to notice that here the writer has tied up the tradition of the promised land to the Zion tradition, that is, the tradition of the city which God has chosen. Actually, this pattern of the use of old election traditions is the general pattern of prophetic eschatology. In summary fashion, it may be said that for the prophets eschatology involves the cancellation of an old election tradition and its replacement with a new one, the relationship between the new and the old being one of analogy in which the new transcends its anticipation in the old.[7] Thus Hosea in chapter 2 refers to a new entry into the land. However, it is Jeremiah among the prophets who deals most extensively with the idea of the return to the land of the promise. This is especially true of the section in his book comprised by chapters 30 to 33. In 30:10 and 30:18 a return is announced, and in 31:4–6 this return is extended to apply to the land of the Northern kingdom:

> Again I will build you, and you shall be built,
> O virgin Israel!
> Again you shall adorn yourself with timbrels,
> and shall go forth in the dance of the merrymakers.
> Again you shall plant vineyards upon the mountains of Samaria;
> the planters shall plant, and shall enjoy the fruit.
> For there shall be a day when watchmen will call
> in the hill country of Ephraim:
> "Arise, and let us go up to Zion,
> to the Lord our God."

Throughout Jeremiah it is the exodus-Sinai covenant tradition which dominates, but in his dealing with the promised return he incorporates to some extent at least the Zion and David traditions as well. Most surprising is the way in which he promises a return of both houses of Israel, "the house of Israel and the house of Judah" (31:27). In 31:38–40 even the "whole valley of the dead bodies and ashes . . . shall be sacred to the Lord." Beginning with a relatively sober oracle as a climax to the symbolic act of the purchase of a field in 32:15—"thus says the Lord of hosts, the God of Israel: 'houses and fields and vineyards shall again be bought in this land' "—an extensive and heavily theological development is made. In 32:36–41 the restoration is promised ("I will bring them back to this place"), but more is involved than physical restoration. The restoration of the covenant relationship is also promised: "They

7. Edzard Rohland, "Die Bedeutung der Erwählungstraditionen Israels für die Eschatologie der alttestamentlichen Propheten"(Dr. Theol. diss., Heidelberg, 1956).

shall be my people, and I will be their God" (v. 38). But the character of this covenant relationship is now revised to a drastic degree: "I will give them one heart and one way, so that they may fear me forever, for their own good and the good of their children after them. I will make with them an everlasting covenant, that I will not turn away from doing good to them; and I will put the fear of me in their hearts, that they may not turn from me" (vv. 39–40). Here the essential change takes place in the nature of God's people so that disobedience is no longer possible. The close analogy to the new covenant passage in 31:31–34 is apparent.

What is involved in such oracles as this? It seems clear that it is the reinterpretation of old traditions that is involved. Some prophets seem to stress one set of traditions and other prophets another set. However, in each case the old tradition forms the analogy for the declaration of the new message. The new covenant will be like the old only greater. However, exodus and covenant were parts of a sequence whose completion involved the entry into the promised land. Thus it is only natural that passages such as Jer. 32:36–41 should climax with the promise of a return to the land: "I will rejoice in doing them good, and I will plant them in this land in faithfulness, with all my heart and all my soul" (v. 41).

The prophet Ezekiel follows a similar pattern in the promises which he declares to his exilic audience. In 34:11–14 he also takes up the theme of the new exodus and new giving of the promised land:

> For thus says the Lord God: Behold, I, myself will search for my sheep, and will seek them out. As a shepherd seeks out his flock when some of his sheep have been scattered on a day of clouds and thick darkness. And I will bring them out from the peoples, and gather them from the countries, and will bring them into their own land; and I will feed them on the mountains of Israel, by the fountains, and in all the inhabited places of the country. I will feed them with good pasture, and upon the mountain heights of Israel shall be their pasture; there they shall lie down in good grazing land, and on fat pasture they shall feed on the mountains of Israel.

A similar message is set forth in 36:8–12 in which the mountains of Israel are addressed as destined once again for habitation:

> I will cause you to be inhabited as in your former times, and will do more good to you than ever before. Then you will know that I am the Lord. Yea, I will let men walk upon you, even my people Israel; and they shall possess you, and you shall be their inheritance, and you shall no longer bereave them of children.

The same type of transformation of the old tradition as in Jer. 31 by which God gives his people that which he has demanded of them, namely the spirit of obedience, is set forth in Ezek. 36:24–28. Once again the promise of a kind of new covenant relationship climaxes in the promise of a new dwelling in the land. This time the tie-up to the promise to the fathers is even more clear: "You shall dwell in the land which I gave to your fathers; and you shall be my people and I will be your God" (v. 28).

The whole variety of traditions can be incorporated in this reinterpretation process. That this is so is illustrated by the incorporation of the "garden of Eden" tradition in a similar promise of restoration in Ezek. 36:35. To a Christian reader it would seem that Ezekiel's message in chapter 37 is the one which should have spoken most vividly to Zionistic hopes of earlier decades. There the elements of despair, longing, and hope are all unified in exceedingly impressive ways:

> Then he said to me, "Son of man, these bones are the whole house of Israel. Behold, they say, 'Our bones are dried up, and our hope is lost; we are clean cut off.' Therefore prophesy, and say to them, Thus says the Lord God: Behold, I will open your graves, and raise you from your graves, O my people; and I will bring you home into the land of Israel. And you shall know that I am the Lord, when I open your graves, and raise you from your graves, O my people. And I will put my Spirit within you, and you shall live, and I will place you in your own land; then you shall know that I, the Lord, have spoken, and I have done it, says the Lord" (37:11–14).

Again, similar to the case in the book of Jeremiah, these promises are extended and expanded to include the restoration of both the kingdom of Israel and the kingdom of Judah (37:21–22). Also at the same time the extension of the promise passes beyond that of physical restoration to spiritual transformation with the assurance:

> I will save them from all the backslidings in which they have sinned, and will cleanse them; and they shall be my people and I will be their God. My servant David shall be king over them; and they shall all have one shepherd. They shall follow my ordinances and be careful to observe my statutes (37:23–24).

In this synthesizing of so many elements from different backgrounds the promise to the patriarchs of the land is not excluded. Verse 25 continues, "They shall dwell in the land where your fathers dwelt that I gave to my servant Jacob; they and their children and their children's children shall dwell there forever; and David my servant shall be their prince forever." Much fusion of traditions takes place in this passage, as the subsequent verses go on to refer to "an everlasting covenant" and a new sanctuary in the midst of God's people through which the nations will come to know that God sanctifies Israel.

It is apparent that what the New Testament writer did in Heb. 11 was simply to follow the lead of earlier generations in a charismatic reinterpretation of past tradition. Like his predecessors the prophets, the writer to the Hebrews did not confine himself to the reinterpretation of one tradition. Among the many such reinterpretations he advances, the one in Heb. 4 particularly deserves our attention because of its relationship to our theme. There the writer picks up the term "rest," which had served both the book of Deuteronomy and Dtr as a technical term. In a highly imaginative synthesis, the writer of the Letter to the Hebrews combines the passage in Ps. 95:11, "As I swore in my wrath, 'they shall never enter my rest' " with the passage in Gen. 2:11, "God rested on the seventh day from all his works." After having referred to the Ps. 95:11 passage in chapter 3 in order to indicate that those who did not enter God's rest failed to do so because of disobedience and unbelief, the writer asserts in 4:1 that "the promise of entering his rest remains," thus contrasting his audience with those of the earlier generation who were unable to enter because of unbelief. In verse 8 the theme is pursued further, when he observes, "If Joshua had given them rest, God would not speak later of another day," referring to the "today" of Ps. 95:11. The reference to Joshua seems to be to such a passage as 21:44 in which Dtr observes that God had given Israel rest. Rather interestingly Dtr advances this statement that God has given Israel rest several times. In 2 Sam. 7:1 it is once again observed in material in the Deuteronomistic history that "the Lord had given him [David] rest from all his enemies round about." And in 1 Kings 8:56 Dtr in an "end-of-era" speech has Solomon pray: "Blessed be the Lord who has given rest to his people Israel." The close connection between the passage in Josh. 21:43–45 and that in 1 Kings 8:56 becomes especially apparent when we notice how each passage climaxes with the claim that not one of God's good promises had failed. This is, however, a highly unusual kind of rest which Dtr finds it necessary to assert as having been given, and yet requiring to be given again and again. The writer to the Hebrews seems simply to continue this pattern of thinking by affirming yet another rest. However, in line with prophetic techniques he goes further and creates a new synthesis by introducing the language of Gen. 2:2 in his claim, "There remains a Sabbath rest for the people of God; for whoever enters God's rest also ceases from his labors as God did from his." Once again, then, we have an eschatological reinterpretation of an old aspect of the theme of the promise and the land.

The earlier noticed terminology of inheritance is not ignored in the New Testament's continuation of the process of reinterpretation. It too is eschatologized and spiritualized in Pauline and related literature. Eph. 1:14 seems to use the term "inheritance" to refer to the fullness of salvation, and it also picks up an old idea by reintroducing the concept of an "earnest," when the Holy Spirit is described as "the guarantee of our inheritance until we acquire possession of it." Verse 18 of the same chapter identifies the inheritance as "the hope to which he has called you" and refers to the "riches of his glorious inheritance in the saints." Col. 1:12 uses extremely similar language as it speaks of "the Father, who has qualified us to share in the inheritance of the saints in light." In what we could now have come to expect as routine procedure for the New Testament writers, the apostle Paul makes additional free use of the inheritance theme when in Gal. 4:1 f. he portrays all the blessings of salvation, especially sonship and freedom, as what the heir receives from his father.

The Subject Today

Just where does all this historical survey lead us? In order even to begin to answer that question it is necessary to analyze from our perspective what it was that took place in the continuing process of reinterpretation which has been noticed. To begin with, as far as I can see, the original promise of a land is never presented to our eyes except as it is taken up in some such reinterpretation. What we term the original promise is available to us only as a hypothetical reconstruction. Our oldest sources clearly engage in the process of reinterpreting this promise so that it applies to their later audience (Solomonic in the case of the Yahwist).

Next, it seems necessary to conclude that all of these reinterpretations have certain traits in common. None of them attempts to convince others who do not share their presuppositions by presenting an argument which will demonstrate the inescapable logical force of their conclusions. Rather than endeavoring to prove, they affirm. Said another way, what these reinterpretations do is to look back, affirming that their present situation constitutes a fulfillment of previous promises, and to look ahead, affirming that the future under God's control will bring no ultimate frustration of those promises. To label such affirmations "proof from prophecy" is to use terminology of an inappropriate sort. Or to attempt today to prove to some disinterested court a legal claim or a historical right of Jews to possess this land on the basis of such passages seems to involve an illegitimate use of them, to say nothing of any efforts to determine boundaries on such a basis. To the same extent, to try to derive secrets of God's timetable for future history from such passages is similarly to violate their intent. What is involved is not proof or prediction, but witness. The connections to midrashic interpretations are obvious.

Still, in order to grasp the significance of this biblical process of reinterpretation with any kind of adequacy it is necessary to explore to some extent the presuppositions of the reinterpreter. He claims to bear witness to the further acts of the same God, but in doing so he displays a high degree of freedom. The way the fulfillment of the promise of the land is switched from the patriarchs themselves to the time of Joshua by the Yahwist and to repeated subsequent eras by Dtr and the prophets illustrates this freedom. The way the gift of the land is attributed to a God who has revealed himself under a different name, Yahweh instead of the former El of the patriarchs, and the way the material reality of the inheritance of the land is spiritualized so that it finds its fulfillment in having God as one's allotment are two particularly clear examples of the extent of this freedom. Because of the theological convictions inherent in the exercise of such freedom, it has been appropriately designated a charismatic freedom.[8] As such it has authority only for those who affirm this charisma of the reinterpreter as valid. Here again any legal use of this material seems clearly excluded.

Perhaps now is the time to ask what charisma these later witnesses claimed to have. The claim of the prophets to speak for God is relatively clear, but what can we say of the Yahwist, Dtr, the psalmists, and the writers of New Testament letters? They simply leave us uninformed about their views of their own authority. In the last analysis, though, this is unimportant. Their authority for us is determined not by their claims, but by the authority we confess to encounter in them, whether

8. Gerhard von Rad, *Old Testament Theology* (Edinburgh, London: Oliver & Boyd, 1965), 2:324 ff.

they advance any claims or not. To the extent that we affirm that these witnesses have authority for us, to that extent we bind ourselves to them. Here, then, comes a point of divergence for Lutherans and Jews, because of the different extent of what we regard as canonical Scripture and our differing attitudes toward subsequent tradition.

The truly "sticky" matters come to light when we ask what kind of charismatic reinterpretation we in our generation attempt in our dealing with the promise of the land. Dare we attempt any such thing? Are we prophets, or even sons of the prophets? It is said "the sons of the prophets are hardy and bold, and quite unaccustomed to fear." In these days it seems appropriate to revise the continuation of that song thus: "But the bravest of all is one, I am told, named Mrs. Golda Meir." But seriously, where are our prophets? We all want to be the sons of the prophets functionally. Our heritage does not prohibit us from such efforts; in fact, it seems rather to demand them of us. The question of what authority we might claim is again irrelevant, since that issue is for those to decide who respond to our affirmations. Not so simple is the issue of the framework of presuppositions from within which we express our affirmations. It was not without considerable forethought that scholars have used the term "eschatology"[9] to describe the character of the prophetic reinterpretation. The extent to which the fulfillments there attested surpassed their anticipations has a bearing on the extent to which the term "eschatology" is applicable. No one, for example, will deny the eschatological character of the transformation of human nature described by both Jeremiah and Ezekiel in their passages about the new covenant and the new heart. Here indeed matters are described which belong to the new era, the age to come. Christians, however, affirm that the New Testament is witnessing to the truth when it affirms that in Jesus the Christ the new age has been inaugurated, although the old age and the new overlap until "the close of the age." Because of this, Christians also affirm that "all the promises of God find their Yes in him [Jesus]" (2 Cor. 1:20). That is to say, about Jesus we confess that in him God himself has "exegeted" his promises.[10] As so many times before, it is from the standpoint of the fulfillment looking back that the character of the fulfillment is affirmed; and again it is affirmed with amazing free-

9. Cf. Rohland *op. cit.* and von Rad, *Old Testament Theology*, 2:113 ff.

10. The phrase comes from Walther Zimmerli, *Israel und die Christen* (Neukirchen: Neukirchener Verlag, 1964), p. 78. Once again it is the case that a new name by which God has revealed himself enters the picture and requires the reinterpretation of previous promises.

dom as transcending its anticipation. Thus, as we have seen, virtually every aspect of every promise—and even many items which never were promises—is attested by the writers of the New Testament as having found fulfillment in Christ. Land, progeny, blessing, new relationship to God, new Israel—these are but a few of the promises which are there taken up and expounded in the light of an affirmed fulfillment. In this connection the promise of the physical land is always spiritualized, but not completely so. The character of New Testament eschatology always maintains the same healthy materialism which inheres in the Old Testament's portrayal of the new Jerusalem. The prominent role of the belief in the resurrection of the body should suffice to suggest what I have in mind.

The character of the freedom exercised in some of these reinterpretations at times seems offensive to us, for it is often quite clear that the fulfillment proclaimed is not in accord with the actual, literal[11] meaning of the promise with which it is connected. That Matthew can find a fulfillment of the deportation of the Northern kingdom—"Rachel weeping for her children" (Jer. 31:15 and Matt. 2:18)—in the slaughter of the innocents is a case in point. For us such connections can have only a homiletical value. And that is exactly the point! From any survey of the usage of "fulfillment" in the New Testament[12] it is apparent that its writers conceived of fulfillment in far broader terms than we. While we are accustomed to associate fulfillment with prediction or at least promise, they clearly used the term to affirm a connection we would label analogy or even merely illustration. Once again, to approach such material by assuming it attempts to offer "proof from prophecy" is to doom oneself in advance to failure in the effort to understand it.

But with all of this hedging taken into account, do any Christian scholars make an attempt to understand the new state of Israel theologically? Specifically, do any such men see here a fulfillment of the promise[13] of God? I know of only one. Walther Zimmerli in his book *Israel*

11. That literal interpretations of these promises involve great difficulties can here be indicated simply by mentioning the problems of the return of the Northern kingdom and a David *redivivus*.

12. See, for example, Brevard Childs, "Prophecy and Fulfillment," *Interpretation* 12 (July 1958): 259 ff.

13. The distinction implied here between *the* promise and *a* promise is important in the thinking of Zimmerli, whose position will be cited below. Zimmerli states that he does "not see how a Christian faith which knows that God's entire word to the world is spoken in Jesus Christ, and that therein also the entire Old Testament promise is fulfilled, can avoid stating that there are no promises or fragments of prophecies left over which are still valid." *Israel und die Christen*, p. 78.

und die Christen points to the apostle Paul's conviction expressed in Rom. 9–11 that the Israel which rejected God's Christ has not thereby been cut off from God's faithfulness. Then Zimmerli continues:

> The Christian church has largely forgotten this preaching of the Apostle. And, therefore, in our day it falls to the lot of the Christian church to be startled by that faithfulness of God which has opposed his merciful history to the human program of a final solution (to the Jewish question).[14]

To be sure, such an affirmation is only a timid beginning. But, it is where we are. And, if we are to go further, it is here and in this way that we must begin.

14. *Ibid.*, p. 80.

6.

The People and the Land

ZWI WERBLOWSKY

The relationship of the Jewish people to the tiny Mediterranean coastal strip known as Palestine is something of a problem: the more theologically minded would even call it a "mystery." It is a relationship that has at all times found expression in certain facts (including traditions, beliefs, attitudes, and actions), and this relationship and these facts begot claims which in their turn resulted in new historic facts. They are part of Jewish history, and understanding them is necessarily part of understanding Jewish history—whether it is the Jew's self-understanding of his historical existence or the gentile's understanding (neutral, sympathetic, or hostile) of this awkward, somewhat irregular, and hence also irritating phenomenon. Part of the total phenomenon to be understood is the fact that for many Jews—including some of the founding fathers of modern Zionism—this relationship and the claims implicit in it were so much taken for granted that they seemed to require no further justification. Understanding the relationship of land and people can be attempted on a purely descriptive and interpretative level, whatever the subsequent conclusions to be drawn from it and even though, for a Jew, the inquiry is inevitably part of his own *prise de conscience* ("existential self-understanding"). It should thus be possible to quote biblical texts not with a view to providing scriptural "proofs" for or against anything, but as illustrations of how the relationship between the people and the land was conceived not only by the authors of the sacred texts, but also by those who interpreted them in their commentaries and homilies, and even by the modern ideologists who quote or echo them, such as the Zionist demonstrators who were protesting in 1939 against the "White Paper" of the British government and carried banners with the legend "Not the British Mandate but the Bible is our title to this land." Our concern, in the present context, would have to be neither with the legal adequacy of the title nor with the logical adequacy of the argument.

Our question would have to be whether that particular claim, though voiced by avowedly secular nationalists, reflects a genuine and authentic continuity of Jewish self-understanding, or whether it is merely a propagandistic gimmick exploiting the nimbus of Holy Scripture. Such an inquiry may require some effort, since it is so much more easy simply to dismiss intangible entities such as the bond between a people and a land, particularly when this bond is a matter of attitudes, emotions, and ideas "only," and when a rival relationship to the same land (that is, actual occupation) by another people can be set against it. But then every nationalism, being nothing but such an irrational bond of "fellow feeling" is easily dismissed as mass hysteria or as a collective *mystique* by well-meaning rationalists as well as by not so well-meaning irrationalists who prefer their own brand of collective mystique.

There is no gainsaying the plain fact that at almost all stages of its recorded existence the Jewish people took its peoplehood (or "ethnicity") for granted. In this respect nineteenth and twentieth century Jewish nationalism presents no new departure but merely the modern articulation of a traditional historical consciousness, differing from the latter only in the sense that modern nationalism differs, by definition, from premodern forms of ethnic consciousness. On the contrary it may be argued that the real departure from traditional consciousness was wrought not by political Zionism but by the movement of religious reform and social assimilation which sought to turn "Judaism" into a denominational entity, organized in synagogues and administered by consistories and similar establishments. It is hardly necessary to add that the Jew's historic consciousness is rooted in his original experience of election, that is, his awareness of the difference of his group in relation to others (the "gentiles"). Whatever the corruptions of which the doctrine of election is capable (and some of them are as surely Jewish corruptions as others are the projection, on the Jew, of unconscious gentile corruptions), it is primarily in terms of difference rather than of superiority that election must be understood. In fact, election is the classical expression, in the language of biblical religion, of what social psychologists today would call a "sense of identity."

This historical self-awareness always contained, as an essential element, a relationship to a particular land. There was, correlated to the chosen people, a chosen, that is, "promised" land. If the Jews are not just a group of people sharing similar theological beliefs, but a people with a specific historic identity—and that is what they consider themselves to be—then the bond to the elect land was part and parcel of their consciousness and religio-national identity.

Like the doctrine of election, the bond to the land could be articulated and rationalized in different ways. At times this bond was "ideal" only: it was experienced in separation and exile, and expressed in the language of eschatological hope. But whether it was actualized in messianic movements or "stored" in liturgical formulae and eschatological expectations, this bond formed part of the total complex of Jewish experience. Some rabbis rationalized the attachment to the land in terms of halakic piety: only in the holy land was it possible to keep God's commandments and fully do his will. To others it was evident that only in the promised land could Israel achieve the spiritual perfection to which it was called. Whatever one may think of a spiritual calling subject to geography, it behooves us to take this tradition for what it is: not only a protest against a disincarnate spirituality, but, more specifically, an unconscious testimony to the inability to affirm any sort of Jewish spirituality other than that of a *people*—it being understood that this people fully realized its existence only in a "hypostatic union" with the land. Traces of this ideology can be found in the earliest strata of biblical literature. Compared to the chosen land, all other countries were impure (Josh. 22:19; Amos 7:17), and to be exiled from the land was tantamount to serving strange gods. At a later date this *mystique* would assume mystico-theosophical forms (as in the Kabbalah) or transform itself into socialist, Marxist, or romantic dreams. Like Antaios in Greek mythology, Israel would draw strength for its rejuvenation and spiritual flowering only from contact with this predestined earth. Rabbinic legend surrounded the land with a halo of superlatives: its fruit was better than that of any other country, and the very fact of dwelling therein had atoning and quasi-sacramental qualities. Where the rabbis left off, popular piety took over: wherever a Jew is buried a handful of dust or earth from the holy land is laid in his grave or coffin. After all, one wants to be buried "at home." But whether subtly rationalized or naively taken for granted, the mystique of this bond was ever present, and only assimilation—in the interests of civil emancipation and in the name of an alleged religious universalism—tried to do away with it. When the reaction set in, partly as a result of acute disillusionment, the bond had perforce to formulate itself in the language of its age and in the light of both the values and the disenchantments to which it was heir. Hence a "secular" vocabulary took the place of the traditional theological one. No doubt this secularization represents a caesura, possibly even a critical break, in the continuity of Jewish history. Yet it is surely no accident that many modern Jewish thinkers could not help resorting to a religious (or "irrational" or "mythological") idiom when seeking to affirm and to explicate the meaning, as they understood it, of the unique relationship between their people and what, through their experience of their people, they also considered as its land.

In the experience of the Jews their relation to the land actually preceded their existence as a people. This may sound like poor logic, but the Lord had said to Abraham "Go from your country, and your kindred and your father's house, to the land that I will show you" (Gen. 12:1). This promise became an "everlasting covenant," as permanent as the laws of nature (Jer. 31:34–35; 33:20–21, 25–26), and the Jews always knew, deep down in their hearts and in the midst of the most abject humiliation, persecution, and massacre, that God would not only remember his covenant with Abraham, Isaac, and Jacob, but that he would also "remember the land" (Lev. 26:42). The notion of a "return" thus became a basic element of Jewish self-understanding and of the interpretation of their existence in exile. Foolishness to Greeks and liberals, and a scandal to Christians, the obstinate Jews persisted in their determination to consider all countries except one tiny Mediterranean coastal strip as the lands of their dispersion. And when—even greater foolishness and worse scandal—they established the state of Israel, this historical event was experienced by them as a "return." Perhaps it is not going too far to suggest that this return was possible because in the historical consciousness of the Jews the bond with their land was consistently formulated in terms of the future. The "land of Israel" is neither a "fatherland" nor a "mother country"; it is the land which God had said he would show to Abraham and give to his seed as an everlasting heritage. In less biblical language we might say that the myth binding people and land together is anchored in the future and not in the past. Perhaps this future-oriented quality of the myth goes a long way towards explaining why even the longest separations could not sever this bond. The crucial point here is not that the Israelite tribe, at some early period of its history, conceived the idea of a promised land, but that this bond, once it had been conceived, persisted even after close to two thousand years of exile with sufficient vitality to become a dynamic and constructive historical factor.

The way the Jews saw it, there always was a mysterious parallelism between their fate and that of the land. For even as they were in exile, suffering ignominy and persecution, so also the land was waste and waiting for the return of its predestined partner. The biblical prophecy (Lev. 26:32) seemed to be confirmed: "I will bring the land into desolation, and your enemies that dwell therein shall be desolate as well." They knew that in the fullness of time God would remember his covenant with his people and remember the land, and meanwhile the actual history of the land, as reported by travelers and pilgrims, seemed to bear out to a remarkable degree the picture they had formed of it. One of the most fertile regions of the ancient world had become a waste and a malaria-ridden area. After the Turkish conquest the desolation of the land reached its peak, and in the nineteenth century, when the population of the world was everywhere expanding, that of Palestine dropped to less than half a million. Hence it is understandable that the impressive achievement of the Jewish pioneers in reclaiming the land and making "her wilderness like Eden, and her desert like the garden of the Lord" (Isa. 51:3) should be perceived, even by convinced secularists, through a halo of biblical associations. In fact, if the land blossomed again this was not merely the result of the heroic and self-sacrificing efforts of the Zionist pioneers in reclaiming malarial swamps and irrigating the desert waste: it was rather—in terms of the traditional Jewish mystique—the response of the Sleeping Beauty to the Prince that had come, at long last, to resuscitate her by his kiss. Whether successful colonization and the transformation of a desert into a garden of the Lord can establish a claim to a territory—claims of this kind have occasionally been advanced by white settlers in Africa—is not the point at all since we are concerned, in the present context, with showing that in Jewish experience the "rebuilding of the land" is the *result* of an anterior relationship and not a cause. As such it confirms a title and does not create one.

Reference has already been made to the curious fact that even in our modern, secular age Jewish thinkers and ideologists are resorting to a religious idiom when trying to explain, to themselves and to others, the meaning of the unique relationship between their people and its land. Some Jewish "Barthians" may repudiate this language as dishonest abuse of a religious vocabulary whose legitimacy requires a definite theological context; others may object to it in the name of a radical Marxism or rationalism. But by and large this religious idiom and pathos assert themselves whenever Jews try to render account unto themselves as to what their historical existence and the land of Israel mean to them.

Among these symbolic expressions and irrational imponderabilia there is one to which Martin Buber has drawn attention. He was referring to the fact that the national renaissance of Jewry "was named after a place and not, like others, after a people." The name *Zionism* indicates "that it is not so much a question of a particular people as such, but of its association with a particular land." Buber's point, in order to be fully appreciated, should be focused even further. The national renaissance of the Jewish people took its name not from a country but from a city. Zion, which since biblical times is synonymous and interchangeable with Jerusalem, serves as a symbol for the country as a whole, and the country is an extension of all that is signified, emotionally and symbolically, by "Zion." The hymn of the Zionist movement, which in 1948 became the national anthem of Israel, speaks of the "eye looking towards Zion" and of the millennial hope of a return to "the land of Zion and Jerusalem." The anthem, known as *ha-Tiqvah* ("Hope") is very poor poetry indeed, but in all its awkwardness and sentimentality it somehow catches the essential—or, if you prefer, the existential—awareness of the Jewish people that at its center there is an indissoluble bond with the land, and that at the center of this center is Zion, the city of David. Jerusalem and Zion are geographical terms beyond mere geography; they are "the local habitation and the name" for the meaning of Jewish existence and of its continuity from the days when God spoke of a certain place that he would choose to the days of the return which—however improbable it might seem—was never in doubt for the Jew.

Alas, to understand a problem is not to solve it. Understanding the nature of Jewish historical existence is, by itself, no answer to the difficulties and conflicts which it encounters and evokes. Legal and political claims can be opposed with legal and political arguments. Historical (or rather "metahistorical") and existential claims can be countered by historical and existential arguments. It is an awkward situation when existential understanding and historic rights are invoked to override rights of a less exalted but all the more concrete order. Meanwhile the millennial Jewish hope and the unshakable Jewish belief in a return have ceased to be mere belief and hope, and have become "concrete" reality. The Arabs saw this new reality taking shape, but were unwilling, perhaps even unable, to understand, and to respond to, the peculiar nature and inner exigencies of Jewish history. They were blind to the historic rights, the background of tragedy behind the Jewish aspirations, the ardor and high idealism motivating them and the constructive achievements resulting from them. The Palestine issue became the symbol and focus of all their failures and frustrations. Hence they resented the Balfour Declaration of 1917 and could not but resist the United Nations decision of 1947 which, for all its involvement in power politics and in Western bad conscience about the Jews, was also an attempt to do justice to the Jewish people and to the unique historical circumstances linking it to Palestine. The Arabs were not prepared to think in terms of relative justice and relative injustice, and to them the justice which the nations of the world did by Israel appeared as *summa injuria*. Seeking the arbitration of violence, the verdict went against them and since then they never wearied of announcing their intention, in words and in deeds, of taking the matter to the court of appeal of further violence. Surely modern Jewry is too secularized—and not presumptuous enough—to describe its repeated victories over the Arab armies in the words of the prophet "Not by might, nor by power, but by my Spirit, says the Lord of hosts" (Zech. 4:6). As a matter of fact all the available might and power were mobilized and deployed, yet no impartial observer can possibly doubt that none of these would have availed without that spirit of profound and absolute inner certainty which is far more than the mere determination of those who fight with their backs to the wall.

Today Israel is no longer a program to be realized or a pious wish to be fulfilled on the basis of hopes, expectations, and biblical promises, or in response to acute persecution of Jews in the diaspora. Israel is a fact, and as far as the Jews are concerned a fact that exists by right of history and not by right of conquest. The conquest was incidental, forced upon the Jews, although—post factum—its importance can hardly be overestimated. Martial ambitions were alien to the Jewish tradition, and the Zionist mythology gave place of pride to the kibbutz, the university, spiritual rebirth, social planning, conquest of nature, but never to war and military glory. Indeed military victory cannot prove a people's right to its land—it is Esau and not Jacob who lives by the sword—but it can prove, and in fact it has proved, Israel's readiness to fight and to die for what it knows with intuitive certainty to be the actual center of its history. Whatever it may be to the outsider, to the Jew the state of Israel, that is, the life of the Jewish people as a body politic in the land which it had never ceased to consider as its own, is not a vain thing newly invented, but a fulfillment that constitutes a further link in a unique historical chain. If we want to borrow from the vocabulary of Christian theology we might say that Jewish existence is an incarnational existence.

Israel, if it takes itself and history seriously, must live the corporate life of a "people," even though it may hesitate to use the term "chosen people" which can sound so presumptuous and lends itself to so many misunderstandings. To deny Israel's right to live its corporate life as a nation is to deny its right to exist. To invite the Jews to live as Jews and to be faithful to "Judaism" without fulfilling their existence in what had previously been defined as the "hypostatic union" of people and land is sheer hypocrisy. The Arabs have made it amply clear that so far they have not intended to discuss modes of coexistence. Their avowed purpose is the "liquidation," "annihilation," and "elimination" of Israel. The Jews require neither the infernal memories of Auschwitz, nor the helpful explanatory clarifications provided by the Arab leaders to realize that these terms mean nothing short of physical extermination and that the announced "politicide" of Israel implies, and is meant to imply, genocide. Israel's life is bound up with its land, the "land of Zion and Jerusalem." Those who appeal to Israel to relinquish this claim actually invite it to relinquish its identity and to commit corporate suicide (or to have themselves massacred once more). It is an appeal so outrageously immoral that Israel can accept it neither from its foes nor from its "friends."

7.

The Doctrine of the Two Kingdoms after Luther in Europe and America

THEODORE G. TAPPERT

The view of the relation of church and state expressed in Luther's two-kingdom ethic has remained an important part of Protestant teaching ever since the Reformation in the sixteenth century.[1] This is not to deny that there have been times during the last four centuries when theologians and others ignored or distorted Luther's formulation, but, generally speaking, the substance of his contention may be said to have retained its place in subsequent thought.

Even during Luther's lifetime Philip Melanchthon, a colleague in the University of Wittenberg, began to introduce modifications. This occurred especially in his later years, when Melanchthon reintroduced the study of Aristotle after joining Luther in the exclusion of the philosopher from theology. The influence of Renaissance humanism was more apparent in Melanchthon than in Luther.[2] The former's lectures and extensive publications on legal and political questions were widely read by contemporary lawyers and jurists and had enormous influence on later generations of theologians as well.

Melanchthon (1497–1560) insisted that a proper distinction must be made between two kingdoms, which he liked to call spiritual and corporeal. The former, he said, was concerned especially with the hereafter, with eternal life, and found its norm in the Scriptures. The latter was concerned with the family, economic life, education, and government and found its norm in natural law. Especially in his later years Melanchthon argued for the introduction of Roman law to replace Germanic law, for

1. Cf. Gunnar Hillerdal, *Gehorsam gegen Gott und Menschen: Luthers Lehre von der Obrigkeit und die moderne evangelische Staatsethik* (Stockholm: Svenska Kyrkans Diakonistyrelses Bok Forlag, 1954), p. 123. Cf. John Tonkin, *The Church and the Secular Order in Reformation Thought* (New York: Columbia University Press, 1971).

2. Adolf Sperl, *Melanchthon zwischen Humanismus und Reformation* (Munich: Kaiser, 1959), pp. 45–170.

he believed that a fixed, written law is to be preferred to an equity achieved by a personally administered justice. There were some differences here between Melanchthon and Luther, but these became sharper when Melanchthon dealt with the interaction of the two kingdoms. The corporeal kingdom (or civil authority) must, he said, provide "the external presuppositions" for the proclamation of the gospel by the spiritual kingdom. These presuppositions included not only the maintenance of order but also the prescription of forms of worship, the education and appointment of clergymen, and the defense of the accepted orthodoxy. In Melanchthon's opinion these *opera externa,* as he called them, naturally belonged to the functions of the state. Civil rulers, called "gods" after Ps. 82:6 and also referred to as "the chief members of the church," were made the custodians of both tables of the decalogue. The way was thus prepared for the development of state churches among Lutherans as among others in Europe.[3]

The differences between Luther and Melanchthon have been incisively put this way by the Methodist historian Franz Hildebrandt:

> First, he [Luther] was always aware of the provisional character of the "Landeskirchentum"; the term "summus episcopus" does not occur in his writings; he was confident that after a period of emergency the church in general council would settle the "reformation." Secondly, he asserted and practiced throughout his life the prophetic office of the church in all public affairs. "Doctor Martinus was asked whether a pastor or preacher had the power to criticize the authorities. Said he: Rather! For although it is God's order, yet God has reserved his right to judge the people and injustice. . . . But it behooves not a preacher to prescribe orders and to teach how dearly bread should be sold or meat taxed." Thirdly, he knew human nature too well to have any illusions about the kingdoms and rulers of this world; a comparison of his personal reflections with those of Melanchthon would show plainly whose was the better psychology *and* eschatology. Lastly, and most important of all, he remained independent of all secular "defensores fidei"; he detested Henry VIII for his assumption of that title; and when his Saxon sovereign would not let him return unprotected from his Wartburg refuge to the dangers of Wittenberg, he gave the classic reply: "I think I could protect Your Electoral Grace more than you can protect me."[4]

John Calvin (1509–64) likewise distinguished two kingdoms and declared in his *Institutes* that "Christ's spiritual kingdom and the civil juris-

3. Guido Kisch, *Melanchthons Rechts- und Soziallehre* (Berlin: DeGruyter, 1967), pp. 19–184.

4. Franz Hildebrandt, *Melanchthon: Alien or Ally?* (Cambridge: Cambridge University Press, 1946), pp. 64–65.

diction are things completely distinct,"[5] although God instituted both and acts through both. It is God's will that civil rulers care for the physical welfare of their subjects and consequently maintain order, protect the weak and oppressed, and punish evildoers. For this purpose they enact and enforce laws parallel to but not identical with the Mosaic law. Civil magistrates are responsible not only for the physical welfare of their subjects, however, for it is also their duty "to cherish and protect the outward worship of God, to defend sound doctrine of piety and the position of the church."[6] Like Melanchthon, Calvin made the civil authority the custodian of both tables of the decalogue and tended to embrace a theocratic view of the state. He also enjoined obedience to bad as well as good rulers, even to tyrants, because the most tyrannical order is to be preferred to anarchy, which is no order at all. Only when commanded to withhold from God the worship due him may a subject resist his ruler.[7] John Knox, a disciple of Calvin and Scotland's reformer, was far less willing to suffer tyranny, allowed recourse to rebellion, and practiced what he preached.

Before we proceed beyond the Reformation we should pause to observe that one of its consequences was to contribute to the independence of the state from control by the church. The process actually began before the sixteenth century, but it was greatly accelerated by the teachings and examples of the Reformers. Powers previously exercised by popes and bishops were appropriated by civil rulers. Often there was a gradual reversal of roles, so that control of states by the medieval church was changed to control of churches by states. We can see this, for example, in the case of King Henry VIII of England and King Gustav Vasa of Sweden. Luther warned against this tendency. A few years before his death, in 1543, he wrote: "We desire that the functions of the church and of the court be kept separate. . . . Satan continues to be Satan. Under the papacy he caused the church to meddle in the state. Now he desires the state to meddle in the church. But with God's help we propose to resist and to do what we can to keep the callings separate."[8] Luther's warning was not heeded. By the seventeenth century Europe

5. John T. McNeill, ed., *Calvin: Institutes of the Christian Religion*, 2 vols., Library of Christian Classics, vol. 21 (Philadelphia: Westminster, 1960), 2:1486 (4.20.1).

6. *Ibid.*, 2:1487 (4.20.2).

7. Wilhelm Niesel, *The Theology of Calvin* (Philadelphia: Westminster, 1956), 229–45.

8. T. G. Tappert, ed., *Luther: Letters of Spiritual Counsel*, Library of Christian Classics, vol. 18 (Philadelphia: Westminster, 1955), p. 345.

entered the age of absolutism in which rulers claimed to govern by divine right and to be above criticism by ordinary mortals. Among the despotic monarchs, significantly, were not only Lutheran and Calvinistic but also Roman Catholic, Eastern Orthodox, and Anglican rulers: Louis XIV of France, Emperor Charles VI of Austria, Peter the Great of Russia, and James II of England. This catalog would seem to demonstrate beyond question that absolutism was less a product of the Reformation than of the Renaissance.[9]

The leading Lutheran theologian at the beginning of the seventeenth century was John Gerhard (1582–1637), and his views were not unsuited to the absolutist rulers of his time. Gerhard and other Protestant theologians of the seventeenth century were influenced both by Melanchthon and by inter-confessional polemics to make Aristotle an authority. Arguments of reason and precedents from history were additional authorities, but Gerhard put his main reliance ostensibly on quotations from the Scriptures. Like his predecessors he distinguished two kingdoms. Each has its own peculiar functions, he wrote, but they also touch each other. The state must provide the order and tranquillity which make it possible for the church to perform its functions effectively, and the church must instill the discipline and morality needed by the state. Of the three forms of government described by Aristotle (monarchy, oligarchy, and democracy), Gerhard unhesitatingly declared monarchy to be the best, and he supported this judgment by citing Aristotle and appealing to analogies in church and family. To the church are assigned *interna* (things that belong to the inner life of man) and to the state are assigned *externa* (things that belong to the relations of groups and institutions to one another). Among the *externa* for which Gerhard specifically made the state responsible were the suppression of heresy, the preservation of orthodoxy, the education and installation of ministers, and the enforcement of Sunday laws. A state may not compel anybody to believe what a church teaches, wrote Gerhard, but it may compel subjects to go to church in order to hear these teachings. Accordingly he made the state the custodian of both tables of the decalogue. Not surprisingly he required obedience to magistrates, no matter what their religious profession and no matter whether they are bad or good rulers. A preacher may reprimand his ruler (on account of his drunkenness, for example), but he must still obey the ruler in *externa*. In all of this we recognize the

9. Werner Elert, *Morphologie des Luthertums,* 2 vols. (Munich: Beck, 1932), 2: 379–95; Heinz-Horst Schrey, ed., *Reich Gottes und Welt* (Darmstadt: Wissenschaftliche Buchgesellschaft, 1969), p. 134.

hand of Melanchthon; even the echoes of Luther are colored by Melanchthon to some extent.[10]

The eighteenth century, which has been called "the sentimental age,"[11] was the time when the movement called pietism flourished. This movement represented a revival of mystical introspection and moral rigor. It had some kinship with the Hassidic movement in Judaism. An unsympathetic historian described pietism as "a spontaneous revival of medieval, monastic piety outside of monasteries."[12] On the positive side pietism represented a revitalization of personal religious experience. Preoccupation with the inner life was accompanied, however, by unconcern with and uncritical acceptance of existing social and political conditions. Often pietists combined a fervent religiosity with a naive nationalism.[13] This helps to explain why some surviving adherents of pietism in the twentieth century greeted the rise of National Socialism as a new revelation and later withdrew into silence.[14]

Many of the Lutherans who found their way across the Atlantic to North America, especially in the eighteenth and nineteenth centuries, were influenced to a greater or lesser degree by pietism and by the scholastic theology of the seventeenth century of which Gerhard was representative. These were part of the baggage they brought with them. In the transition from the old world to the new the most obvious adjustment Lutheran colonists and immigrants had to make, whether they came from Scandinavian, German, or other lands, was the replacement of state churches with free churches and an acceptance of pluralism. As before, however, they continued to distinguish between law and gospel and to hold that God rules through church and state. In the teachings of the Reformer they found support for the separation of church and state and for the principle of voluntarism in religion which developed in North America.

Although there were shifts of emphasis during the last four centuries there was a return, again and again, to the insight of the Reformation concerning the teaching of the two kingdoms. This happened, to take a couple of recent examples, during the confessional awakening of the

10. Ernst Uhl, *Die Sozialethik Johann Gerhards* (Munich: Kaiser, 1932), pp. 87–131.

11. Max Wieser, *Der sentimentale Mensch im 18. Jahrhundert* (Gotha, 1924).

12. Albrecht Ritschl, *Geschichte des Pietismus,* 3 vols. (Bonn: DeGruyter, 1880–86), 2: 417.

13. Koppel S. Pinson, *Pietism as a Factor in the Rise of German Nationalism* (New York: P. S. King & Son, 1934), pp. 180–206.

14. Reinold von Thadden, *Auf verlorenem Posten?* (Tübingen, 1948), pp. 45–55; Hartmut Lehmann, *Pietismus und weltliche Ordnung in Württemberg vom 17. bis zum 20. Jahrhundert* (Stuttgart: Kohlhammer, 1969), pp. 334–35.

nineteenth century and during the so-called Luther Renaissance of the twentieth century. Despite some modifications, the two-kingdom ethic was not seriously challenged in Lutheran or Calvinistic circles until Karl Barth attacked it in 1938 in his essay, "Rechtfertigung und Recht."[15] Amid the disillusionment and bitterness in Europe on the eve of World War II Barth gave currency to the mythology that Luther stood at the beginning of a straight line that extended through Frederick the Great and Bismarck to Hitler.[16] Actually Luther had helped free the state from ecclesiastical encroachment when he placed it under God's creation; Barth placed it under God's redemption, as had been done in the Middle Ages. To this the Congregational historian Wilhelm Pauck responded by pointing to Barth's confusion of law and gospel and by writing: "I do not find Barth's doctrine of the 'righteous state' acceptable. . . . It is derived from his concept of revelation and thus placed on too narrow a base. This opinion can be proved, it seems to me . . . by the fact that he cannot find a proper interpretation of the Soviet state."[17]

It would be foolhardy to suggest that Luther's two-kingdom ethic was uniformly apprehended and applied during the past four centuries. It would be presumptuous to contend that alongside of other powerful forces which have been at work in shaping history—economic realities, nationalistic sentiments, geographical considerations, military might, ambition, pride, prejudice, propaganda, and the like—a theological affirmation has prevailed all by itself. But it would probably not be too much to say that the two-kingdom ethic has pointed toward acceptable political and ecclesiastical stances, especially in times of crisis.

15. Hillerdal, *Gehorsam gegen Gott und Menschen,* pp. 8–9.
16. Schrey, *Reich Gottes und Welt,* p. 130.
17. Will Herberg, ed., *Community, State, and Church: Three Essays by Karl Barth* (New York: Doubleday, 1960), p. 67.

8.

Lutheran Theology and the Third Reich

URIEL TAL

I would like to limit myself to one issue that has become, because of the Jewish experience during the twentieth century, the focus for any discussion of the interrelationship of theology and political responsibility. This critical issue is the relationship of Lutheran political theology to the Third Reich, and consequently to the Holocaust.

Before presenting a Jewish view of the interrelationship between the theology of the kingdom of God and the Third Reich, I should like to make a methodological and epistemological observation. Jewish contemporary thought, including theology, has undergone a deep change during recent years. The ontological categories of our thinking on this issue are not the same ones we used in pre-Holocaust times. While the Holocaust occurred in history, in contemporary Jewish thought it has assumed a dimension which is metahistorical; while it happened to human, physical beings, its significance today is seen not in physical, but in metaphysical, terms. Though it was an event, or an act, committed by a political state, it is understood in a metapolitical way, one which has a meaning beyond the limitations of time, of space, of causality, or of any other category of reason.

This change in the structure of our thinking emerged on two levels. The first is a purely philosophical level, as pointed out by Emil Fackenheim. Accordingly, after Auschwitz there can be no validity anymore to Hegel's doctrine that "rationality" and "actuality" are identical.

The second change was on the level which concerns us here, the historical level. Historically, the change in the structure of post-Holocaust thinking originates in the Third Reich itself. In the Third Reich, as well as in the entire tradition of the *Kulturpessimismus* from the middle of the nineteenth century on, a radical transformation of values took place, a change from metaphysics to the realm of the physical, from God to man, from religion to myth, from symbolism to realism. This transformation of values took the form of a return to the worship of life and might, of sun, mountains, rivers, and forests, as the National Socialist Student Federation proclaimed in 1934, quoting nineteenth century Romanticism: ". . . Germanic soil . . . the promised land, the kingdom of priests and the holy *Volk* . . ." By reversing the meaning of historical traditions, Nazi mythology exalted man, that old pagan Adam, which it called *das Urmenschliche im Ur-Germanen* ("the archetype of humanity in the primal German"), as spiritual man, as the son of God in whom the German is transformed into "a new creation" as in Wilhelm Stapel's exegesis of Gal. 6:15 and 2 Cor. 5:17. The German would be freed, as Hans Schomerus taught, by overcoming death, that is, by overcoming the Judaic roots of Christianity, of Western civilization, of liberalism, rationalism, and of their origin, the Jew.

The Holocaust as such remains, at least in our day, incomprehensible. Yet forms of thought and action which paved the way towards the Holocaust may perhaps become, if not understood, then at least explicable. From a methodological point of view the thought structure which seems to have been crucial was the process of transformation, of transfiguration, of a total reversal of meanings. Values that in monotheism and consequently in Western civilization had previously been regarded as relative, now became absolute; and values that had formerly been considered absolute and were incorporated in the web of religious life by means of sacraments, metaphors, or allegories, now became relative. Means were converted to ends, and ends were endowed with absolute authority to justify means. Freedom was interpreted not as freedom for, but as release from, the scrutiny of reason, the restraint of logic, or the normative restrictions of personal responsibility.

Consequently the theological understanding of the two kingdoms was secularized and politicized.[1] Man, the Adam—and his archetype the Jew —was transfigured from a person, a subject created in the image of God and endowed with inalienable rights, into an object, deprived of his divine image and natural status, and thus doomed to be annihilated. This transformation of ontological categories, and the Jewish reaction to it, are at the core of contemporary trends in Jewish thought on the issue we are discussing here, which is religion and statehood, the earthly kingdom and the kingdom of God, in short, the history of political interpretations of

1. Cf. the fundamental work by Wolfgang Tilgner, *Volksnomostheologie und Schöpfungsglaube. Ein Beitrag zur Geschichte des Kirchenkampfes* (Göttingen: Vandenhoeck und Ruprecht, 1966), Part Two, pp. 88 ff.

the coming of the kingdom of God: "The time is fulfilled, and the kingdom of God is at hand" (Mark 1:15; cf. Matt. 4:17).

This aspect of the Holocaust is explicitly responsible for many phenomena in contemporary Jewish life, such as the so-called obsession of the Israelis to defend themselves and stubbornly survive on the one hand, and on the other the consistent reluctance of many young Israelis to surrender to the temptations of power, or to rejoice at the defeat of their military opponents, lest "he who hates his neighbor will shed his blood in the end."[2] Consequently, the contemporary Jew and Israeli have found relevance in the way Christians have morally and politically wrestled with the delicate differentiation between Rom. 13:1–6 and Rev. 13, or with Luther's doctrine on temporal authority, and on the kingdom of God and the kingdom of this world, or with Luther's interpretation of divine authority.[3]

For once, the Jew—and Israeli too—is mighty, a citizen of his own sovereign state; like his Christian neighbor, he has to come to terms with both power and justice, or political responsibility and theology (1 Pet. 2:17). Consequently there is a renewed interest nowadays in studying the implications of Luther's teachings on the right and duty to disobey (*des Ungehorsams*), to protest, and even to rebel against an unjust political regime (*Unrechtsstaat*), and also on the authoritarian structure of society and state in which "*etliche frey seyn, etliche gefangen*" ("some are free, some are imprisoned").[4]

It is the hope of most Jews not to learn from the example European Christendom has provided in its history; yet for the first time since the destruction of Jerusalem in A.D. 70, we too are experiencing power and the danger that its use may turn into abuse. Nowadays Judaism, too, is confronted with the dilemma between a fundamental approach to biblical prophecies and their spiritualization, as was recently discussed by a group of young Israel-born students of history. In order to justify Zionism, they asked, should we too utilize "proof texts" among the prophetic visions of

2. Babylonian Talmud *Ketuboth*, 77/6.

3. Martin Luther, *Von weltlicher Obrigkeit, wie weit man ihr Gehorsam schuldig sei* (1523), in *D. Martin Luthers Werke. Kritische Gesamtausgabe* (Weimar, 1183–), 11:(229) 245–280, hereafter cited as *WA*; cf. "Temporal Authority: To What Extent It Should Be Obeyed," in *Luther's Works*, ed. Jaroslav Pelikan and Helmut T. Lehmann, 56 vols. Concordia, St. Louis and Philadelphia, Fortress Press, 1957–), 45:81–129, hereafter cited as *LW*. *Ein Sendbrief von den harten Büchlein wider die Bauern* (1525), *WA* 18:(375) 384–401; cf. "An Open Letter on the Harsh Book Against the Peasants," *LW* 46:63–85.

4. Martin Luther, *Ermahnungen zu Frieden* (1525), *WA* 18:(279) 291–334, esp. 327; cf. "Admonition to Peace," *LW* 46:39.

the Messiah, such as: "Rejoice greatly, O daughter of Zion, shout, O daughter of Jerusalem, behold thy king cometh unto thee. He is triumphant and victorious" (Zech. 9:9), the way Christians have justified their creed: "Now this happened in fulfillment of what was said by the prophet" (Matt. 21:5; John 12:14)?

Is it possible to maintain the spiritual meaning of God's kingdom, that creation itself will be delivered out of its enslavement to corruption, and into the freedom of the glory of the sons of God (cf. Rom. 8:21), and at the same time apply this meaning to political reality, one in which physical power with all its temptations is unavoidable, as taught by Article XVI of the Augsburg Confession on civil government (*De rebus civilibus; von der Polizei und weltlichem Regiment*)?

It is this context that makes the study of the two kingdoms of such a vital importance to all of us.

William H. Lazareth in "The Church as Advocate of Social Justice"[5] and Theodore G. Tappert in "The Doctrine of the Two Kingdoms after Luther in Europe and America"[6] have emphasized that the Third Reich misinterpreted and misapplied Luther's doctrine of the two kingdoms, and that it would thus be wrong to claim a straight, simple line from Luther to Hitler, or from the traditional political quietism of Lutherans to the acceptance of the yoke of dictatorship. Nor would it be correct to assume that the two kingdoms doctrine preaches an ethical double standard, thereby making possible or even permitting the godless autonomy of the state.

I support this contention of Lazareth and Tappert. Any interpretation of Luther's theology as the direct causal factor that inevitably brought about Nazism does not bear the scrutiny of factual, objective research. Jewish and Israeli scholars, as part of our contemporary scientific study of Judaism (*Wissenschaft des Judentums*) were among the first historiographical schools to refute such oversimplified approaches. Salo W. Baron, in his illuminating *Modern Nationalism and Religion*[7] asserted as early as 1947 that the historical roots of Nazism in the nineteenth century included also anti-Christian elements. Hence, despite official declara-

5. William H. Lazareth, "The Church as Advocate of Social Justice," *Lutheran World* 28, no. 3 (1971): 245–269, esp. p. 253.

6. Theodore G. Tappert, "The Doctrine of the Two Kingdoms after Luther in Europe and America," pp. 81–86 above.

7. Salo W. Baron, *Modern Nationalism and Religion* (New York: Harper & Row, 1947).

tions on the merits of "Positive Christianity,"[8] once it reached its full power Nazism recognized the church as one of the most dangerous enemies of racism, of Hitler's political aims, and of Alfred Rosenberg's *Mythus.*[9] Recent historical research sustains Baron's fundamental conclusion.[10] It is obvious that to many of the fathers of the racial and political anti-Semitism that emerged during the last quarter of the nineteenth century and culminated in the Holocaust, the rejection of Judaism was tantamount to the rejection of all religion, including Christianity.

Modern racial anti-Semitism discovered that religion and moral conscience had their roots in Judaism, as Hitler told Rauschning;[11] therefore, Nazism also turned against the fruit born of those roots, with entirely different methods and consequences, of course. Nazism objected to the restraining influence of Rev. 13 as well as to Luther's statement that civil disobedience is allowed if the ruler commits ungodly violence.[12] Starting with Eugen Duhring, most influential leaders of racial anti-Semitism and of Nazism up to 1945 negated the theology of the sovereignty of God's kingdom whereby there are "all things in Christ both which are in heaven and which are on earth" (Eph. 1:10), and transformed it into an atheistic and mythological ideology. As Alfred Rosenberg in a paraphrase of Rev. 22:12–13 proclaimed: "From now on a new era of salvation [*Heil*] has begun, not God the Lord but Hitler the Führer is the Alpha and the Omega, the first and the last, the beginning and the end."[13]

However, while any attempt to draw a straight line from Luther to Hitler would certainly distort historical truth, the same approach to history does indicate the need for a careful consideration of a dialectical development between authoritarian trends in the Third Reich and political implications of Luther's "Temporal Authority." As Reinhold Nie-

8. Cf. the program of the National Socialist German Workers' Party, section 24, and the excellent study by John S. Conway, *Die Nationalsozialistische Kirchenpolitik* (München: Kaiser Verlag, 1969), pp. 160 ff. (Cf. Conway's *The Nazi Persecution of the Church, 1933–45* [New York: Basic Books Inc., 1969].)

9. Alfred Rosenberg, *Der Mythus des 20. Jahrhunderts; eine Wertung der seelisch-geistigen Gestaltenkämpfe unsrer Zeit* (München: Hoheneichen Verlag, 1930).

10. Cf. my *Religious and Anti-Religious Roots of Modern Anti-Semitism*, Leo Baeck Memorial Lecture, No. 14 (New York: Leo Baeck Institute, 1971).

11. Cf. Eberhard Jackel, *Hitlers Weltanschauung—Entwurf einer Herrschaft* (Tübingen: Wunderlich Verlag, 1969), chap. 3, pp. 58 ff.

12. See Ernst Wolf's *Barmer-Kirche zwischen Versuchung und Gnade* (Munich: Kaiser Verlag, 1970), pp. 137–49.

13. Cf. the *Kirchenkampf* archives of Bielefeld, Germany, Section M, photostated at the Cisler Library, Wayne State University, Detroit.

buhr in his *Christianity and Power Politics*[14] said as early as 1940, the history of Nazi pessimism with its glorification of force as the principle of order, its unqualified affirmation of the state and its earthly interpretation of the kingdom of heaven, could not be understood without the early history of the Lutheran Reformation.

This dialectical process in which theology negated itself developed during the Third Reich in two different movements. Both drew sustenance from the same theological sources, such as Rom. 13:6 and especially its "Lutheran" interpretation. Contrasted were those who by the power of God's free will are redeemed and consequently subject only to spiritual authority (*geistliches Regiment*), with those who are not citizens of the celestial kingdom, that is, heretic, unchristian, evil, or non-Christian people, for whom God has ordained worldly political authority, the power of the sword *(weltliches Regiment)*. At the same time, the two movements strongly opposed each other. One of them was the confessing church (*Bekennende Kirche*) inspired by Karl Barth, exemplified by Dietrich Bonhoeffer and Helmut Gollwitzer and led by men such as Martin Niemoller, Heinrich Vogel, Heinz Gruber, and Bishops Wurm, Dibelius, and Lilje. The other consisted of the Protestant Nazis who in the middle of 1937 united their various groups, established the national church movement of "German Christians" (*Deutsche Christen*) and proclaimed: "Christ is not the source and fulfillment of Judaism, but its deadly adversary and conqueror."[15] Many of the members of the second movement were disciples of theologians such as Wilhelm Stapel, Hans Schomerus, and Emanuel Hirsch, with faith in the saving power of the Führer who "redeemed the Aryan from the power of the sword" (*Regiment des Schwertes*).[16]

At first sight, here were two different, antagonistic movements. The confessing church opposed totalitarianism and fought against what it called the deification of political leadership, against the sanctification of blood and soil, of state and might, against the pseudomessianic structure of Nazism as reflected in the eschatological authority bestowed upon nationalism, imperialism, and statehood. In one of the first widespread

14. Reinhold Niebuhr, *Christianity and Power Politics* (New York: Charles Scribner, 1940).

15. Cf. Kurt Meier, *Kirche und Judentum—die Haltung der evangelischen Kirche zur Judenpolitik des Dritten Reiches* (Göttingen: Vandenhoeck und Ruprecht, 1968), p. 31.

16. Cf. *Kirchenkampf* archives; cf. also Franklin H. Littell, *The German Phoenix* (New York: Doubleday, 1960), chap. 1: "From Barmen to Stuttgart."

protests against both Nazism and racial anti-Semitism of March, 1935, the Old Prussian Confessing Synod proclaimed: "We consider our nation threatened by a deadly danger. The danger is represented by a new religion."[17]

On the other hand, the "German Christians" supported Nazism and its policy whereby the state and the party used dogmas of sin and salvation to convert men into loyal subjects. The essential belief of Christianity, that man is saved through faith in the forgiveness of Jesus who died for man's sins "so that the sinful body might be destroyed and we might no longer be enslaved to sin" (Rom. 6:6), was transferred from the theological to the secular, political plane. The Pauline teaching in 1 Tim. 1:9, subsequently reaffirmed by Luther, that the law is not given to the righteous man but to the unrighteous, was transformed from the spiritual plane to racism. The righteous man, who according to Luther transcends physical, political law, now equalled the Aryan, and the rest—those ungodly, unchristian, sinful and lawless men who according to Luther are subject to the law and the sword—now embodied and symbolized by the Jew, were doomed not simply to be punished but destroyed, annihilated.

Among the yet unpublished documents that were collected by the late Professor Karl Thieme we find the following revealing statement, issued by the Thuringian "German Christians" led by Leffler and Lentheuser: "I learned about the divine source of political authority from Rom. 13:1, from Augustine's *City of God* and from Luther's "Temporal Authority." . . . From John 1:14 I learned that . . . the word became flesh and dwelt among us. . . . It then suddenly hit me as a new revelation, that if the word is flesh, and the whole fullness . . . dwells bodily (Col. 2:9), the realm of God too must have been transfigured into an earthly city. Man became God and Christ continues to act through our Führer. . . . The entire universe is redeemed from the bondage of the law, of the spirit, of moral restrictions derived from petrified Talmudism . . . in this redeemed cosmos there can be no longer any place for the arch enemy of our revolution, the Jew . . ."

Despite these extreme contrasts, both of these two contradictory movements attempted to apply "Lutheran" solutions to the Jewish question. One (the confessing church) acknowledged the right of the Jew to exist physically, but primarily so that (following "That Jesus Christ Was Born

17. Meier, *Kirche und Judentum*, p. 29.

a Jew," 1523)[18] he might be saved spiritually. The other (the "German Christians") negated the right of the Jew to a proper, normal, human existence. In any case he would not be saved and therefore is doomed to remain subject not to the heavenly part of the kingdom (where people who believe in John 18:36 ff., Matt. 4:17; 6:33; 24:14 belong), but to authority and the sword (following "On the Jews and Their Lies," 1543).[19]

The confessing church, from the very beginning, fought against the persecution of Jews, but primarily of baptized Jews, the so-called "non-Aryan Christians." Though Jews were more than once protected by individual Christians, the nonbaptized were rarely, if ever, included in the struggle of the confessing church, except for a few protests such as that by Helmut Gollwitzer in his sermon on the Day of Repentance on November 16, 1938.

As we study the rich documentation on the *Kirchenkampf* ("church struggle"), we are impressed with the following fact: while the church raised its voice against the persecution of the Jews out of humanitarian motives, as well as in the hope of thereby strengthening its own members, the traditional dogmatic concept of the Jew continued to be dominant. According to this view the persecution of the Jews is an error, not only for reasons of humanity, but mainly because persecution prevents the Jew from seeking redemption among his persecutors. It prevents the Jew from accepting Jesus as the Messiah and from seeking in the New Testament that salvation which not only is promised him, but without which Christianity itself is doomed to remain unfulfilled. From the theological point of view regarding the right of Judaism to exist, the church in its protest against the Nazis reverted to the original attitude of Luther, as expressed in "That Jesus Christ Was Born a Jew" of 1523. When Luther protested against the anti-Jewish policy of the Roman church, claiming that the church treated the Jews "as if they were dogs"[20] and that under such circumstances he himself would "sooner have become a hog than a Christian,"[21] his protest was not based on an acknowledgment of the right of Judaism to exist as an independent, autonomous religion. The motive that inspired this protest was the hope that Christianity would mitigate the persecution of the Jews and apply to them

18. *LW* 45:199–229; cf. *WA* 11:(307) 314–36, *Das Jesus Christus eyn geborner Jude sey.*

19. *LW* 47:137–306; cf. *WA* 53:417–552, *Von den Jüden und ihren Lügen.*

20. *LW* 45:200.

21. *Ibid.*, p. 200.

instead the Christian commandment of love and tolerance: "If some of them should prove stiff-necked, what of it? After all, we ourselves are not all good Christians either."[22] In that case, and only in that case, Christians might hope that the Jews would return and believe in the salvation brought to them by their own Messiah.

Against this historical background, Christianity apparently continued to identify the Jews even during the Holocaust not in their own authentic terms, but according to the classical tradition. The Jew is a person who persists in the impenitent rejection of Christ, and who must be saved, for it is the Jew who has to complete the eschatological process of salvation history (*Heilsgeschichte*). Therefore Jews, and especially converts, have to be rescued from racial discrimination. Moreover, since Judaism continues to be an integral part of Christianity, the very notion of the Jews as a race can have no basis whatsoever in Christian theology.[23] This was stated as early as September, 1933, by the theological faculty of the University of Marburg in its statement against the "Aryan paragraph." Similar statements were issued in 1934 by theologians such as Rudolf Bultmann and the members of a confessing group located in Bethel, Germany.[24] Thus, even at the height of Nazi persecution and while the extermination of the Jews was proceeding, the church did not acknowledge Judaism as a religion in its own right and on its own terms, but insisted that a Jew who became a Christian was merely fulfilling his predestined role. Such a Jew did not leave his faith: he returned to his true faith.

It is most symptomatic and instructive to note that in the controversy between Heinrich Vogel (one of the leaders in the protest against the persecution of Jews and the author of *65 Theses of Protest*, March, 1933) and Friedrich Gebhart (a spokesman of the "German Christians" who wrote a *Reply* to the *65 Theses*, May, 1933), both sides, despite their theological and political contradictions, adhere to the same traditional Christian view that the Jews are in a state of rejection (*Verwerfung*). One view holds that the Jew can abrogate his old covenant and step over to the side of the redeemer; the other holds that the derelict Jew is beyond salvation and the redeeming influence of the church, that *Ueberzeugung* ("conviction") cannot overcome *Zeugung* ("race"). Both,

22. *Ibid.*, p. 229.

23. Cf. *Der Ungekundigte Bund*, ed. Dietrich Goldschmidt and Hans-Joachim Kraus (Stuttgart: Kreuz-Verlag, 1963), p. 206.

24. *Ibid.*, p. 218.

however, despite the far-reaching differences and contradictions between them, deny the Jew the right to live on his own terms and according to his own self-definition.

The interrelationship of Lutheran political theology and some of the authoritarian trends in the Third Reich teach us that there is no determinism in human history. Luther's call for a reaffirmation of a divinely ordained civil authority and at the same time for true faith so that men shall no longer need the worldly authority since "the Kingdom of God is in the midst of you" (Luke 17:21) has been both used and abused.

Its abuse contributed to the emergence of German racial authoritarianism, while a highly moral interpretation of Lutheran teachings on the two kingdoms was given by men such as Dietrich Bonhoeffer. It is this interpretation that may put into a new historical perspective instructive documents such as the statement of the Lutheran Church in America which proclaims "this forbids any state from deifying itself."[25]

25. From the Social Statement, "Church and State: A Lutheran Perspective," adopted by the Third Biennial Convention, Kansas City, Missouri, June 21–29, 1966.

PART THREE

HOW WE SPEAK OF GOD TODAY

9.

How to Speak about God in a Pluralistic World

GEORGE W. FORELL

Perhaps the most dramatic difference between, on the one hand, the writers of the Hebrew Bible and the Lutheran fathers who wrote the confessions and later constructed the baroque edifice of Lutheran Orthodoxy, and on the other, modern Jews and Lutherans and their twentieth century contemporaries, is the different way in which they and we speak about God. It is obvious to the psalmist that "the heavens declare the glory of God; and the firmament showeth his handiwork" (Ps. 19:1). And to question God's existence is a demonstration of self-evident, empty-headed foolishness: "The fool hath said in his heart, 'There is no God' " (Ps. 14:1; cf. Ps. 53:1), and "Foolish people have blasphemed thy name" (Ps. 74:18). Therefore: "Arise, O God, plead thine own cause: remember how the foolish man reproacheth thee daily" (Ps. 74:22).

The orthodox Lutheran fathers could speak of "innate" and "acquired" knowledge of God and John Quenstedt claimed that "the *natural knowledge of God* is that by which man, without any special revelation, may know of himself, though very imperfectly, by the light of Nature and from the Book of Nature, that there is some supreme Divinity, and that He, by His own wisdom and power, controls this whole universe, and that He has brought all things into being."[1] John Gerhard says, "*Innate knowledge* is that common conception concerning God engraven and impressed upon the mind of every man by Nature."[2]

It is part of our common experience as twentieth century people that the denial of the existence of God does not demonstrate either the foolishness or the inhumanity of a person. Indeed some very intelligent and

1. John Quenstedt, *Theologia Didactico-Polemica* (1685), 1:251, quoted in Heinrich Schmid, *Doctrinal Theology of the Evangelical Lutheran Church*, 3rd ed. rev. (1899; reprint ed., Minneapolis: Augsburg Publishing House, 1961), p. 105.

2. John Gerhard, *Loci Theologici* (1621), 1:93, quoted in Schmid, *Doctrinal Theology*, p. 105.

humane contemporaries, some of them self-consciously Jewish, others self-consciously Christian, have felt it incumbent upon them to claim, "There is no God," or even more dramatically, "God is dead!"

It is this obvious change in our situation which raises the question, "How can we speak about God in our pluralistic world?" Perhaps Peter Berger's commonsense definition of pluralism offers a helpful beginning for our discussion. He describes the contemporary situation with the following words: "Subjectively, the man in the street tends to be uncertain about religious matters. Objectively, the man in the street is confronted with a wide variety of religious and other reality-defining agencies that compete for his allegiance or at least attention, and none of which is in a position to coerce him into allegiance. In other words, the phenomenon called 'pluralism' is a social-structural correlate of the secularization of consciousness."[3]

Both Jews and Christians have reacted negatively to the reality of pluralism in their past history. The preferred solution for both traditions was a land in which there would be no adherents of false gods to lead the followers of the true God astray. About the Hivites, the Canaanites, and the Hittites, we read: "You shall make no covenant with them and their gods. They shall not stay in your land for fear they make you sin against me, for then you would worship their gods, and in this way you would be ensnared" (Exod. 23:32, 33). The religion of the true God did not tolerate competing "reality-defining agencies." Similarly, Luther wrote in the preface to his most popular and widely read and studied work, *The Small Catechism* of 1529, to "all faithful and godly pastors and preachers": "If any refuse to receive your instructions, tell them that they deny Christ and are no Christians. . . . Parents and employers should refuse to furnish them with food and drink and notify them that the prince is disposed to banish such rude people from his land." And Luther continued, "Although we cannot and should not compel anyone to believe, we should nevertheless insist that the people learn to know how to distinguish right and wrong according to the standards of those among whom they live and make their living."[4] As late as the sixteenth century it seemed obvious to almost everybody that the moral and religious standards of a community were both knowable and unequivocal—*almost* everybody, for by then the Jewish experience was significantly

3. Peter L. Berger, *The Sacred Canopy* (New York: Doubleday, 1967), p. 127. Copyright © 1967 by Doubleday & Company, Inc. Reprinted by permission.
4. Martin Luther, *The Small Catechism*, in *The Book of Concord*, ed. Theodore G. Tappert (Philadelphia: Fortress Press, 1959), p. 339.

different. The days of the religiously homogeneous Jewish kingdom were long gone, if they ever existed anywhere but in the pious imagination, and Jews had to pioneer the arduous experience which characterizes modern man, namely, to be a cognitive minority, to be people with a discrete perspective among an alien majority. What set the Jews apart in Europe since the beginning of the Constantinian era is now the common experience of all men and women of faith. They are all cognitive minorities who look at the world from a perspective which is not shared by the majority. It would be my claim that we must learn from our Jewish neighbors how to maintain our idiosyncratic perspective in a pluralistic world. No longer supported by *cuius regio eius religio* ("whose the region, his the religion") or even a *consensus gentium* ("agreement of nations"), we must learn to maintain our faith in a world whose dominant plausibility structures are not supportive of our faith, but are either neutral or inimical.

In order to speak of God in this kind of world, the complexity of the religious reality must be kept in mind.

(1) There is more to being a Christian than intellectual assent to certain Christian propositions. Jews always knew that there is more to being a Jew than making a Jewish confession of faith. In a pluralistic world all must learn as much. Christians in general, and American Lutherans in particular, have frequently overemphasized the cognitive aspect of faith, as if the symbols we use to speak about God were the reality itself. Some of the controversies among Christians about the nature of God seem to assume the accessibility of information about him that is simply not available to mortal man. Not satisfied to see through a mirror dimly, we claim to see face to face, and Eastern and Western Christians, for example, were divided by the *filioque* phrase in the Nicene Creed, claiming to know definitively that the Spirit proceeds from the Father or from the Father and the Son, as the case might be. The cognitive aspect of our religion is important and inescapable. One cannot be a Christian without the assent to certain propositions, as for example, "God was in Christ, reconciling the world to himself" (2 Cor. 5:19). Whether there are such minimal propositions for all people who accept themselves as Jews, I cannot judge. But Christianity is far more than such assent, and in the kind of world in which we live, we must be careful not to speak about God in such a manner that he merely becomes a proposition to which we assent.

(2) But there is also more to being a Christian than the adoption of

and adherence to a moral code. Religion has indeed a moral dimension. It implies a way of life, a style of life. Christianity has frequently been understood by those on the inside as well as those on the outside as a life lived according to certain moral precepts. They may be as detailed and specific as those governing the everyday existence of an Amish farmer. They may be as vague as the exhortation of the follower of "situation ethics" to do the most loving thing. In either case those who see religious reality in general and the Christian faith in particular as obedience to one, few, or many commandments, also fail to see the complexity of the Christian faith. The reality of the threat of legalism will not be denied by anyone who has studied Protestant or Roman Catholic moral theology and is familiar with the example from one text, published in America in the last generation, which claims that masturbation is a greater sin than rape—since the former is basically counter to nature, while the latter is not. But it is really only a quantitative and not a qualitative difference between this monstrous type of legalism and the agapeic calculus advocated by the new morality, which allegedly enables us to determine with complete certainty in respect to every action whether it is "good" or "evil."

Again, our Jewish brothers and sisters are familiar with the problem of pan-halakism, "which regards *halacha* [law and tradition] as the only source of Jewish thinking and living."[5] As the late Professor Heschel writes: "In justification of their view, exponents of religious behaviorism cite the passage in which the Rabbis paraphrased the words of Jeremiah (16:11), *They have forsaken Me and have not kept My Torah,* in the following way: 'Would that they had forsaken Me and kept My Torah.' " And Heschel continues, "However, to regard this passage as a declaration of the primary if not exclusive importance of studying Torah over concern for God is to pervert the meaning of the passage. Such perversion is made possible by overlooking the second part of the passage, which reads as follows: 'Since by occupying themselves with the Torah, the light which she contains would have led them back to Me.' "[6] This warning against pan-halakism, whatever its status in the Jewish community, is of the greatest importance for Christians. Those who today say "There is no God, but Jesus is his Son,"

5. Abraham Heschel, *God in Search of Man* (New York: Meridian Books, 1959), p. 328.

6. *Ibid.*, pp. 329 ff.

who would replace orthodoxy with their evolutional or revolutionary orthopraxis, do not help us to speak meaningfully to a pluralistic world. Indeed, what we do is important. As Luther put it succinctly, "God threatens to punish all who transgress these commandments. We should therefore fear his wrath and not disobey these commandments. On the other hand, he promises grace and every blessing to all who keep them. We should therefore love him, trust in him, and cheerfully do what he has commanded."[7] But this does not mean that we can speak of God today as the giver of eternal laws, as the great computer in the sky, if we lean in the direction of fundamentalism, or as the inexorable process of history through which justice works itself out with the help of dialectical materialism, as those who lean in the direction of neoliberalism, or the so-called radical theology would have it. The God of the Bible is a God in search of man, who desires that we accept our acceptance though we know ourselves to be unacceptable (Tillich).

(3) But there is also more to being a Christian than an emotional experience or the feeling that, "I am okay and you are okay." There can be no doubt that an overwhelming experience is at the heart of the Christian speech about God. If there is no experience there is no power. It is the experience of the disciples which makes them eloquent; it is the experience of Paul which compels him to speak. Again Luther says, "I believe that by my own reason or strength I cannot believe in Jesus Christ, my Lord, or come to him. But the Holy Spirit has called me through the Gospel."[8]

It is this awareness of a divine call, of an encounter or at least a "feeling of absolute dependence" (Schleiermacher) which enables the Christian to say "*I* believe," and not only "The church believes." But the Jewish experience seems not to be radically different. The Hebrew Bible is full of experiences of encounter with God which are decisive and determinative for those who are exposed to them. They have become models for Jews and Christians. And this prophetic experience is seen as transcending all knowledge, all philosophy, by Moses Maimonides: "Prophecy is a different source and category of knowledge. Proof and examination are inapplicable to it. If prophecy is genuine then it cannot and need not depend on the validation of reason. The only test ever asked of a prophet in the Scriptures is concerning the genuineness of his

7. Luther, *The Small Catechism*, p. 344.
8. *Ibid.*, p. 345.

claim to have prophecy, but no one ever asked for proofs or reasons or validations above prophecy itself."[9]

But for Christians and Jews experience is qualified. Not every powerful emotional experience is the encounter with the God of the Bible. Sincerity of emotion is not enough. We, who live in an age when unspeakable crimes are being committed by utterly sincere fanatics and where almost every day brings news from all over the world of deeds of vicious violence in the name of patriotic or religious emotions, or a horrible combination of the two, must be particularly insistent upon the content and result of religious experience. When Luther spoke about the work of the Holy Spirit in *The Large Catechism*, he said: "To this article, as I have said, I cannot give a better title than 'Sanctification.' In it is expressed and portrayed the Holy Spirit and his office, which is that he makes us holy."[10] Thus the experience is a sanctifying experience, or, again in Luther's words, "We come to love and delight in all the commandments of God because we see that God gives himself completely to us, with all his gifts and his power, to help us keep the Ten Commandments: the Father gives us all creation, Christ all his works, the Holy Spirit all his gifts."[11] Indeed there is such a thing as Christian experience, but it is sharply focused. It is not morally neutral, it helps us to live lives of love, i.e., to obey the commandments.

It would appear to me that Rabbi Heschel speaks of a similarly qualified experience when he writes: "What gave the prophets the certainty that they witnessed a divine event and not a figment of their own imagination? The mark of authority of the divine character of revelation was not in outward signs, visible or sonorous; revelation did not hinge upon a particular sense-perception, upon hearing a voice or seeing a light. A thunder out of a blue sky, a voice coming from nowhere, an effect without a visible cause, would not have been enough to identify a perception as a divine communication. . . . This, it seems, was the mark of authenticity: the fact that prophetic revelation was not merely an act of experience but an act of *being experienced*, of being exposed to, called upon, overwhelmed and taken over by Him who seeks out those whom He sends to mankind. It is not God who is an experience of man;

9. Maimonides in a letter to Rabbi Hisdai, quoted in Heschel, *God in Search of Man*, p. 233.

10. Martin Luther, *The Large Catechism*, in *The Book of Concord*, ed. Tappert, p. 415.

11. *Ibid.*, p. 420.

it is man who is an experience of God."[12] Certainly experience is central to the speech about God in a pluralistic world. If we speak without reference to experience we will seem incredible to an experience-oriented age. But not every experience will do. False prophets are more common than prophets of the living God and religious experience can now be obtained in the drug store or in an encounter group. If we speak about God in terms of experience in our pluralistic world we must say that valid experience is not absolute but qualified by righteousness and holiness.

(4) And finally, there is more to being a Christian than the sense of belonging to the Christian community. In our pluralistic world the importance of religion as an aid to personal and sociological identification has assumed ever greater importance. In an age in which the reality of pluralism offers so many possibilities, the problem of identity has assumed increasing significance, especially for the young who see these options more clearly and thus feel more threatened by what the existentialist would call a "dreadful freedom." Obviously it did not involve any great effort for a Lutheran Swede at the end of the nineteenth century to accept himself as a Lutheran. There was actually little else he could do. For his descendant living in America at the end of the twentieth century to do the same is something vastly different, because he now has a genuine choice. If he accepts himself as a Lutheran Christian, he identifies himself with a certain historical and cultural tradition, and this identification rather than any belief in certain theological propositions, a particular moral outlook, or specific emotional experiences may be the reason for his decision. Because of the human need for roots, the importance of the remembrance of things past in order to establish one's identity, the communal aspect of the Christian faith has assumed new significance. A person suffers from amnesia if he does not know who he is, and this happens when he cannot remember anything about his past. And such amnesia is ever more common. People do not know who they are because they do not know where they came from, because they have forgotten their pasts.

It is the increasing awareness of the resulting isolation and estrangement which makes speech about the God who calls people into a community meaningful to rootless and isolated human beings in a pluralistic world. Speaking about God to this world means to speak about him who calls the "solitary into families." Luther said: "I believe that there

12. Heschel, *God in Search of Man*, pp. 229–30.

is on earth a little holy flock or community of pure saints under one head, Christ. It is called together by the Holy Spirit in one faith, mind, and understanding. It possesses a variety of gifts, yet is united in love without sect or schism. Of this community I also am a part and member, a participant and a co-partner in all the blessings it possesses."[13]

It is clear that for Luther, belonging to this community is a great source of strength and that he sees the gifts of God coming to him and to all Christians as members in this community. To be a Christian means to belong to a community. Just as in the New Testament the term "saint" (*hagios*) does not occur in the singular but always in the plural, so it is impossible to be a Christian in splendid isolation. This notion, which may strike an individualistic and autistic age as primitive and perverse, should not seem surprising to Jews who have always said that "Jewish faith consists of attachment to God, attachment to Torah, and attachment to Israel."[14] Indeed the experience of Jews as a minority in an alien world has anticipated the pluralistic development where all religions experience themselves as minorities in a world in which the majority sees everything differently. Here we may learn both the opportunity and the danger of this situation.

Indeed, we are called to community but the community which God's call establishes is a community for the world. The church exists not for itself but for the service of the world. We belong to the church only if we lose ourselves in service to mankind. Again the similarities to the Jewish self-understanding are obvious. "The future of all men depends upon their realizing that the sense of holiness is as vital as health. By following the Jewish way of life we maintain that sense and preserve the light for mankind's future visions. It is our destiny to live for what is more than ourselves."[15] It isn't just any community Jews and Christians speak about but a community of service to mankind. In order to speak about God in a pluralistic world in the light of the communal dimension of the Bible, it is not enough to speak about sociological and personal identity and identification. Any community from the Boy Scouts to the Ku Klux Klan and from the Rotary Club to the John Birch Society may supply some such meaning. Christians must be a disciplined community. When they speak about God they must speak about the God who wants a people to serve him. Community is qualified by holiness.

13. Luther, *The Large Catechism*, p. 417.
14. Heschel, *God in Search of Man*, p. 425.
15. *Ibid.*, p. 424.

We spoke of the complexity of the religious reality. If we are to speak of God in a pluralistic world all aspects of the religious reality must be taken seriously—the cognitive dimension, the moral dimension, the emotional dimension, and the communal dimension. But none of them are enough in themselves. We have often been misunderstood because we have isolated one of these dimensions and emphasized it out of all proportion and made it dominate our speech. But they all belong together. When any of them is missing our speech about God is falsified and thus misleading. In a pluralistic world all kinds of people will be attracted and repelled by various aspects of our speech. This is as it should be. Some who may be repelled by theology might find community helpful, some who abhor emotion may cherish the moral dimension. In the pluralistic world in which it is our destiny to live, we will do best to mention all the dimensions of God's reality as we see it. But because he is the God of reason as well as righteousness, of feeling as well as community, we will hope that these dimensions are not seen as mutually exclusive and thus falsified. We will also remember that even the most eloquent human speech about God remains *human* speech subject to all the frailties to which man is heir. It is only when God himself uses our speech for his purposes that he will speak so that people will be able to hear even in a pluralistic world. That God be heard in spite of and through our human speech is our hope and prayer.

10.

Judaism, Ecumenism, and Pluralism

MARC H. TANENBAUM

In his perceptive study, *The Social Sources of Denominationalism*,[1] Richard Niebuhr argued that the religious diversity in American society during the first half of the twentieth century represented not so much theological differences as the accommodation of Christianity to "the caste system" of human society. He declared that social factors played a decisive, negative role and were largely responsible for the disunity of American Christendom. Elaborating his thesis, Professor Niebuhr asserted that the religious proliferation of the denominations and sects closely followed the division of men and women into castes of national origins, race, class, and sectional groups which constitute the American society. In short, the pluralism of America undergirded and reinforced the diversity of religious behavior.

Three decades later, quite paradoxically, another Christian analyst employed the identical categories of Professor Niebuhr and arrived at opposite conclusions. Robert Lee wrote in his book, *The Social Sources of Church Unity,* that during the decade of the 1950s and thereafter, social factors made a positive contribution to the rise of ecumenism and Christian unity. He observed that church unity springs from the growing cultural unity within American society.[2] Dr. Lee posited the emergence of a *homo americanus*—a "consensus American."[3] There was an increased awareness of a common frame of reference in which Americans tended to see things from a similar perspective. Dr. Lee cited the social changes in race, class, sectionalism, and nationalism as factors contributing to the emergent cultural unity. There was now "a common culture" based on a shared universal education, a common language, economic well-being,

1. H. Richard Niebuhr, *The Social Sources of Denominationalism* (New York: Henry Holt and Co., 1929).

2. Robert Lee, *The Social Sources of Church Unity* (Nashville: Abingdon Press, 1960), p. 17.

3. *Ibid.,* p. 23.

growing intermarriage between members of denominations and faiths, the establishment of national cultural symbols through the influence of the culture-producing mass media, and an evolving network of mutual dependence through the organizational revolution which is the basis of our urban, industrialized civilization. Cementing this social and cultural unity, Dr. Lee wrote, were the unifying influences of "common value themes," most notably, a shared belief in individualism, freedom, democracy, and success.

Whether or not social forces advance or inhibit unity between religious groups is a subject worthy of continued examination and reflection. One conclusion emerges inescapably, however, from the studies of Professors Niebuhr and Lee, and that is the basic fact that neither ecumenism, nor interreligious relations, nor pluralism can be adequately comprehended solely on "spiritual" or "doctrinal" grounds. A comprehension of "extra-theological" factors is critical for a genuine understanding of the complex reality of such vital relationships.

What are some of the extratheological realities that constitute the matrix of the current ecumenical and interreligious scene? A portrait of that matrix has been sharply sketched by Professor Zbigniew Brzenzinski of Columbia University, who writes in his study, *Between Two Ages*:

> The paradox of our time is that humanity is becoming simultaneously more unified and more fragmented. That is the principal thrust of contemporary change. Time and space have become so compressed that global politics manifest a tendency toward larger, more interwoven forms of cooperation, as well as toward the dissolution of established and ideological loyalties. Humanity is becoming more integral and intimate even as the differences in the condition of the separate societies are widening. Under these circumstances, proximity, instead of promoting unity, gives rise to tension prompted by a new sense of global congestion.[4]

Another preeminent feature of current extratheological reality that influences in decisive ways ecumenical and interreligious relationships is depicted by the Dutch theologian and social scientist, Dr. Anton C. Zijderveld, who writes in his book, *The Abstract Society*:

> The structures of modern society have grown increasingly pluralistic and independent of man. Through an ever enlarging process of differentiation, modern society acquired a rather autonomous and abstract nature

4. Zbigniew Brzenzinski, *Between Two Ages: America's Role in the Technetronic Age* (New York: Viking Press, 1970), p. 3. Copyright © 1970 by Zbigniew Brzenzinski. Reprinted by permission of The Viking Press, Inc.

> confronting the individual with strong but strange forms of control. It demands the attitudes of obedient functionaries from its inhabitants who experience its control as an unfamiliar kind of authority. That means societal control is no longer characterized by a family-like authority but dominated by bureaucratic neutrality and unresponsiveness. The individual often seems to be doomed to endure this situation passively, since the structures of society vanish in abstract air if he tries to grasp their very forces of control. No wonder that many seek refuge in one or another form of retreat.[5]

He adds:

> Modern society has become abstract in the experience and consciousness of man! Modern man, that is, does not "live society," he faces it as an often strange phenomenon. This society has lost more and more of its reality and meaning and seems to be hardly able to function as the holder of human freedom. As a result, many modern men are turning away from the institutions of society and are searching for *meaning, reality* and *freedom* elsewhere. These three coordinates of human existence have become the scarce value of a continuous existential demand.[6]

These two authors reinforce a shared conviction about what is the paradoxical and contradictory predicament in which the contemporary person finds himself and herself. The planetization of the human family through electronics, automation, instant mobility, and satellite communications has made mandatory that everybody adjust to the vast global environment as if it were a global city. At the same time, that globalization of the human consciousness has led to the undermining of dependencies on the more limited local loyalties, such as the nation-state. The effects of that are to be seen especially among our young people, many of whom feel a weakened sense of national patriotism and have little emotional fervor about national sancta and rituals, while feeling very much at home roaming Europe, Asia, Africa, and Latin America as if they were born as natural citizens of the world. To many of them, the global city is already a dominant fact of contemporary life.

The human situation is complicated by the fact, however, that those of us who live in the advanced Western societies based on scientific and technological foundations confront bureaucracies and vast organizations as the crucial and all-pervasive structures through which we sustain all

5. Anton C. Zijderveld, *The Abstract Society* (New York: Doubleday and Co., 1970), p. 11.

6. *Ibid.*, p. 54.

the material conditions of our existence. And as Zijderveld indicates, the dominance of these bureaucracies in our lives has resulted in a profound identity crisis. By and large we do not dominate these structures, rather they control us. We have very limited roles in decision-making in these vast systems. Our functions are generally partial, fragmentary, frequently frustrating, leaving most of us with little sense of mastery or control or direction over this large segment of our lives. In the pursuit of personal meaning, a desire for wholeness, and for clarity about one's identity, it is no accident that there has emerged in recent years such a spontaneous growth of youth communes, encounter and human potential movements. On another level, this search for identity is also reflected in the growth of ethnic group self-assertion, and in the support of denominationalism rather than interdenominationalism, which is perceived as abstract and distant from personal and direct communal needs. The identity quest is also a factor in the movement of peoplehood among blacks, *la Raza* among Spanish-speaking groups, "red power" among American Indians, and the mystique of peoplehood and mutual interdependence among Jews throughout the diaspora and in Israel. There is evidently a vast yearning for human-size communities in which the individual can relate to another person on a face-to-face basis, in an environment of caring, shared concern, and mutual confirmation.[7]

If this analysis of our situation is reasonably accurate, albeit sketchy, what then are some of its implications for ecumenism and interreligious relations today and tomorrow? I suggest that the following issues are involved and deserve our priority attention.

The emerging transformation of the planet into a global city makes it mandatory that we establish some living connections for ourselves and for our young people between our theologies, our religious teachings, and the realities of the emerging unity of the human family as well as its pluralism. Never before in human history, in my judgment, have Judaism and Christianity had an opportunity such as the present one to translate their biblical theologies of creation—the unity of mankind under the fatherhood of God—into actual experience.

This extraordinary, indeed unprecedented, moment of potential fulfillment of biblical ideals and values has become obscured for us by the dominance of uncritical tendencies to sloganize that we live in a "post Judeo-Christian era," a "post-Western age," a "postmodern era." The

7. See "Do You Know What Hurts Me?" by this writer, *Event* 12 (February 1972): 4–8 (published by the American Lutheran Church Men).

effect of such doom-and-gloom slogans is that they tend to become self-fulfilling prophecies, contributing to the paralysis of insight and will. If we would penetrate to the reality beneath the slogans, we could justifiably conclude in fact that we are in a "*pre*-Judeo-Christian era." There are evidences supporting such a conclusion all around us if we will insist on careful analysis rather than allow ourselves to be seduced by faddist catchwords.

It is no accident that the most dramatic advances in science and technology have taken place in the Western world. The decisive impact of the biblical world view on Western civilization, in particular the Genesis teachings on creation, have resulted in the "disenchantment" of nature—to use Max Weber's concept—which enabled biblical man to subdue and master nature for human purposes, an absolute precondition for scientific and technological experiment. Further, the biblical theology of redemption contributed to a messianic conception of history, which conditioned biblical man to responsibility for the events of history.[8]

In nonbiblical cultures, religions, and societies, this linear view of history leading to messianic redemption does not prevail. Rather the cyclical views of history have by and large resulted in passivity and quietism, preconditions for indifference to poverty, illness, and illiteracy. If history is fated to repeat itself as an endless cycle, what reason exists for seeking to alter the course of history?

As nations in the third world have begun to come to grips with the magnitude of human suffering and deprivation in their midst, and to embark on economic development and nation-building, it is evident that they will have to appropriate science and technology as the instruments for producing the food, clothing, medicine, and shelter for meeting their basic human needs. The third world nations will be able to mediate the benefits of Western scientific-technological technics, I contend, only if they make some fundamental accommodations to the Western, hence Judeo-Christian, assumptions and categories regarding nature and history, as well as toward man, society, and God. That means that a genuine convergence must perforce take place in which the Jewish and Christian *Weltanschauung* becomes central and formative in the construction of a universal technetronic civilization.

The moral and spiritual challenge to Judaism and Christianity in that convergence process will be as acute as the culture shock for Oriental

8. For a fuller discussion of this issue, see my essay, "Some Current Mythologies and World Community," *Theology Digest* 19 (Winter 1971): 325.

religions and civilizations will inevitably be. The temptations to repeat triumphalisms, imperialisms, and monopolies of truth will have to be resisted mightily by the bearers of Western scientific cultures into the third world. The need to help preserve the integrity of non-Western cultures and religions, their rich inheritances of spirituality and inwardness, and not to allow these legacies of mankind to become obliterated by the machines of science and technology becomes all the more evident with every passing day.

Thus, a primary issue on the agenda of the human family is that of helping build a united human community that respects diversity and difference as a permanent good, quite clearly as a God-given good. We must confess, however, that based on present evidence we are far from adequately prepared either theologically or humanly to realize this delicate and essential balance of unity in the midst of diversity.

To the development of such a theology of human unity and pluralism I would hope that Judaism, in dialogue with Christianity and Islam and other world religions, would make a special and distinctive contribution. It is not widely known that there is available a substantial body of Jewish doctrine and teaching which, though composed over the past three thousand years, contains ideas, conceptual models, spiritual and human values of surpassing insight and meaning for our present situation. Let us review briefly some of the highlights of what is called "the Jewish doctrine of the nations of the world—*ummot ha olam*," which today we might well call the Jewish doctrine of pluralism—and world community.

The relationship of the people of Israel to mankind takes as its first and foremost principle the fact that, according to the Torah, all men are descended from one father. All of them, not as races or nations, but as men, are brothers in Adam, and therefore are called *bene Adam*, sons of Adam.

From the time of the occupation of the promised land of Canaan down to the present day, the treatment of every stranger living in the midst of an Israelite community has been determined by the commandments of Mount Sinai as recorded in the book of Exodus: "And a stranger shalt thou not oppress, for ye know the heart of a stranger, seeing ye were strangers in the land of Egypt" (Exod. 23:9).

In the extensive biblical legislation dealing with the stranger, the *ger* ("sojourner") or the *nokhri* ("foreigner")—whom you are to love as yourselves (Deut. 10:19)—are equated legally and politically with the Israelite.

From the first century of the present era and thereafter, the "stranger within the gate" in the diaspora who joined in the Jewish form of worship but without observing the ceremonial laws, became known as a *yire adonay*—a God-fearer. A God-fearer was one who kept the Noachian principles, that is, the moral principles known to Noah and to pre-Israelite mankind. As described in the Babylonian Talmud (*Sanhedrin* 56), the seven commandments of the sons of Noah are these: the prohibition of idolatry, of blasphemy, of sexual immorality, of murder, of theft, of cruelty to animals, together with the positive commandment to establish courts of justice.

The great twelfth century Jewish philosopher, Maimonides, formulated the normative Jewish conception, held to and affirmed by all periods of Judaism (in *Mishnah Torah IV, Hilkot Melakhim,* Section X, *Halachah* 2) in these words: "Whoever professes to obey the seven Noachian laws and strives to keep them is classed with the righteous among the nations and has a share in the world to come." Thus every individual who lives by the principles of morality of Noah is set on a par with the Jews. Indeed, a statement made by Rabbi Meir (ca. 150 C.E.) is recorded three times in the Talmud, "The pagan who concerns himself with the teaching of God is like unto the High Priest of Israel" (*Sanhedrin* 59a; *Baba Kamma* 38a, and *Aboda Zara* 36a).

Thus, this rabbinic doctrine about "the righteous men among the nations" who will be saved made it unnecessary, from the point of view of the synagogue, to convert them to Judaism. At the same time, it should be acknowledged that Jews pray daily in the synagogue for what appears to be the ultimate conversion of the gentiles not to the cult of Israel but rather to the God of Israel: "Let all the inhabitants of the world perceive and know that unto thee every knee must bend and every tongue give homage. Before thee, O Lord our God, let them bow down and worship, and unto thy glorious name let them give honor."

While there is no unanimity in Judaism regarding the ultimate conversion of the gentiles, there can be no doubt that, theologically speaking, Judaism does expect a redeemed mankind to be strict monotheists—in the Jewish sense. It is the duty, therefore, of every Jew to encourage both by teaching and personal example the universal acceptance of the "Seven Principles of the Sons of Noah." The ultimate conversion of the world is understood by Judaism to be one of the "messianic" events. We will know that the messianic age has come when we realize a change—a conversion—in the kind of life being lived on earth, and not just in the inner life of the individual. Wars and persecutions must cease, and justice and peace must reign for all mankind.

Translating this religious language into contemporary terms, Judaism affirms that salvation exists outside the synagogue for all who are God-fearers, that is, all who affirm a transcendental reality as a source of meaning for human existence, and who also live by the moral code of the sons of Noah. This Jewish theological view also perceives and undergirds world pluralism as a positive good. Thus Judaism advocates a unity of mankind which encourages diversity of cult and culture as a source of enrichment, and that conception of unity in the midst of diversity makes possible the building of human community without compromise of essential differences.

The central issue of teaching about the unity of mankind raises the pedagogical problem: How do we teach commitment and loyalty on the part of our youth and adults to one's own faith, and at the same time recognize, respect, and even reverence the claims to truth and value of religious traditions outside our own?

Critical for the management of that vital task is the need to face the inadequacy of much of our current theological and philosophical understanding of the meaning of "unity" and the implications of such understandings for religious liberty and freedom of conscience in a pluralistic world. The weight of much Western ideological and religious thinking and experience is shaped by the imperial theologies and ideologies that governed Europe from the fourth until the early nineteenth century. At the request of his friend Emperor Constantine, Bishop Eusebius of Caesarea conceptualized perhaps the earliest Western version of "imperial theology" when he linked monotheism with the concept of the Roman emperor: "one God, one empire, one church." That led Walter Ullmann to observe in his *History of Political Thought,* "The ancient pagan idea of the Emperor as 'Lord of the World' reappeared in the Christian universal idea of rulership. It was not only his right but also his duty to spread Christianity and hold together the Ekumene, the totality of all cultured peoples, by means of the Christian faith."[9]

In the sixteenth century Reformation, the enforced unity of faith and nationalism was manifested in the imperial doctrine of *cuius regio eius religio* ("whose the region, his the religion"). By his act of uniformity and supremacy, Henry VIII brought the church and commonwealth under

9. Walter Ullmann, *A History of Political Thought: The Middle Ages* (Baltimore: Penguin Books, 1965), pp. 32–33.

his civil power, thus realizing in the English Reformation the medieval philosophy of unity. In the United States, Martin Marty has described in his book, *The Righteous Empire*, how the first half century of American national life saw the development of evangelicalism, which "set out consciously to create an empire, to attract the allegiance of all people, to develop a spiritual kingdom and to shape the nation's ethos, mores, manners, and often its laws."[10]

Two British churchmen, whom Marty cites, after their visit to America in 1836 declared, "Blot out Britain and America from the map of the world, and you destroy all those great institutions which almost exclusively promise the world's renovation." On the positive side, they added, "Unite Britain and America in energetic and resolute cooperation for the world's salvation, and the world is saved."[11]

This evangelical and Anglo-Saxon tradition equated the American way of life, the defense of laissez faire capitalism, and the crusade against communism with the Christian mission to the world. "So close was the fusion between the American republic with evangelicalism," Marty writes, "that a basic attack on American institutions meant an attack on Protestant Christianity itself. Positively, the defense of America meant a defense of the evangelical empire."[12]

In the second, more recent, period of American history, the ecumenical moderates tried to extricate the Protestant churches from identification with the American way of life, from a single economic pattern, and from a crusading spirit. They tried to break way from the provincialism and chauvinism of their fathers who equated the kingdom of God with the evangelical empire. They sought to become an experiencing agent in the nation and not merely the dominant molder of symbols. They reached back to other elements in the American constitutional tradition and supported a pluralism whose ground rules were that "no religion was to have a monopoly or a privileged position and none should be a basis for second class status for others."[13] That tradition of liberal Protestant pluralism has made possible the Christian ecumenical dialogue and the Jewish-Christian dialogue. The dialogue means that people could have exposure to each other across the lines of differing faiths without attempting to convert in every encounter, without being a threat, and

10. Martin Marty, *The Righteous Empire: The Protestant Experience in America* (New York: The Dial Press, 1970), p. 17. Copyright © 1970 by Martin E. Marty. Reprinted by permission of The Dial Press.

11. *Ibid.*

12. *Ibid.*, p.

13. *Ibid.*, p. 253.

with the hope that new understanding would result. The goal would be a richer participation in the city of man, the republic, or the human family.

The presuppositions of that ecumenical approach to pluralism and to Jewish-Christian relations involved at its deepest levels a fundamental theological and philosophical reconceptualization of unity. One of the clearest formulations of that revised rethinking of unity is reflected in the words of the Protestant theologian Herbert Richardson, who wrote in his book, *Toward An American Theology*:

> By direct henological analysis, we can attain to the conclusion that the unity of everything that exists is (1) the unity of any denumerable individual or individuality; or (2) the unity of any two or more individuals when taken together, or considered as one thing—i.e. relationality, or (3) the unity of any or all possible relationalities considered as complete or wholeness.
>
> From this analysis, it seems that every unity (whether it be an individual, a relation, or a whole) is as real as any other unity. This means not only that each individual is, from the metaphysical point of view, as real as any other individual, but that any individual is as real as any relation, or any whole, including the whole which encompasses all things. Or, to say it another way, "the universe" is no more real than any individual within the universe—for the characteristic of reality is unity, and it is as real to be an individual as to be a whole. While a "whole" is "bigger" than certain individuals, it is not ontologically of a higher grade, i.e., not better. Moreover, a whole does not add to or subtract from the reality of the individuals existing within it. These have their own independent principle of being (their unity of individuality) and so they are *a se* and not from the whole. . . . Individuals have their own being within the whole, but from themselves, for individuality does not originate in, nor derive from wholeness, nor the reverse. Wholeness, individuality, and relationality are therefore three distinct hypotheses of unity. As such, each is capable of being the principle of an independent system of categories.[14]

That recasting of a philosophical understanding of unity is experienced in our awareness of the many languages of mankind. The many languages and varieties of humankind are not something to overcome in a quixotic pursuit to bring mankind to speak one language. That does not mean that the many languages do not influence and change each other; they do. The multiplicity of languages points to the many-sided conversation which is required. That conversation distributes the varieties of human

14. Herbert Richardson, *Toward An American Theology* (New York: Harper & Row, 1967), p. 82.

gifts and types; and it is as we gain the capacity to listen and speak, to hear and respond even though we will be changed that our one humanity comes into existence.

The conception of the unity of the whole as not being ontologically "better" than the unity of the parts which compose it also has implications for the Jewish-Christian relationship. Rosemary Ruether, the Catholic theologian, has noted that "Christianity, as the fulfilled universalism of a particularism, could not tolerate the continued contrary particularism (i.e. the individuality) of the Jew."[15] She further elaborates that:

> gentile attitudes toward Jews are unalterably fixed by the totalistic universalism of a Christian fulfilled messianism. Such a Christian theological stance demands, in some form, the drawing of a mental ghetto of negation around those who reject this fundamental Christian self-affirmation.[16]

"A Christian assertion," Dr. Ruether adds, "that Jesus is 'the Messiah of Israel,' which contradicts the fundamental meaning of what Israel means by 'Messiah,' is and always has been fundamentally questionable."

> That questionableness must now be clarified and unambiguously applied to the historic sin of its translation into the negation of the Jews. This demands a relativizing of the identification of Jesus as the Christ. Contextually, we can speak of Jesus as the "messianic experience for us," but that way of speaking doesn't make this experience self-enclosed: it points beyond itself to a liberation still to come.
>
> Both the original roots of Christian faith and the dilemma of modern Christology will make it evident that such an affirmation of the messianic event in Jesus in a contextual and open-ended rather than a "once-for-all" and absolutistic way, is demanded by the existence of Christian theology itself. In this way the Christian experience can parallel rather than negate the liberation experiences that are the community symbols of other faiths. For the Jews, the Exodus experience is also a very actuality of liberation that is, at the same time, a hope for liberation still to come. In this way the Jew and Christian stand in parallel traditions, each having tasted grace, each looking for a fulfillment that is "beyond."[17]

In effect, Dr. Ruether employs the Jewish-Christian relationship as microcosmic illustration of the macrocosmic theological problematic.

15. Rosemary Ruether, "Christian Anti-Semitism and the Dilemma of Zionism," *Christianity and Crisis,* 17 April 1972, pp. 91–92.

16. *Ibid.,* p. 94.

17. *Ibid.*

The reality and urgency of reconceptualizing inherited categories whose exclusivistic and imperial tendencies paralyze Western religious communities in an effort to respect the claims to truth and value of the non-Western world's religions is graphically illustrated in the writings by Father Tissa Balasuriya, OMI, of Colombo, who declared in "The Church and Change in Asia":

> In the last eight to ten years the concept of the salvific value of these religions (of Asia and Africa) also is gaining ground. It is now admitted that Christians too can learn something regarding God and salvation from the other religions. In the last 3–4 years the concept of salvation of individuals and even nations is giving way to the idea of a world mission in which every people has to learn and can teach something to others. Salvation is being understood as more closely related to justice and the building of the fraternal community of man on earth. This is the Kingdom of God, of which institutional churches are signs and means—sacramental expressions. Though the theory of the mission has changed among the more advanced Christian groups, the old mentality still largely prevails in practice.[18]

In summary, there are two opposing conceptions of world community that are now being contested on the global scene. In a world in which two-thirds of the human family is neither white, nor Jewish, nor Christian, a refurbished Western evangelicalism, reinforced by Anglo-Saxon *hybris*, can be the surest way of leading to disaster on a global scale. If we have learned anything worthwhile from the American experiment, and particularly from the Jewish-Christian dialogue, it is the knowledge that Jews and Christians are learning to live together as brothers and sisters, are seeking to build community without compromise of their respective differences, and are learning to celebrate the wisdom that unity in the midst of diversity may after all be the will of God.

If Judaism and Christianity can grant the validity of each other's covenants, and seek to affirm the best in each other rather than deny it, there need be no reservation about their fruitful coexistence. Indeed the two covenants could be seen in the divine scheme of things as mutually complementary, not mutually exclusive. The very concept of the "covenant of the sons of Noah" demonstrates that Judaism did not limit God's covenanting to the Jews. The new covenant, as I understand St. Paul in Rom. 9 to 11, does not revoke the old. Both covenanted communities have after all for some two thousand years uttered the same prayer,

18. Father Tissa Balasuriya, "The Church and Change in Asia," *Commonweal*, 29 June 1973, p. 354.

"Thy kingdom come." And when the kingdom comes, when the Jew sees the fulfillment of the prophecy, "The Lord shall be king over all the earth; in that day the Lord shall be one, and His name one" (Zech. 14:9), the Christian, too, will see the fulfillment of prophecy. "Then comes the end, when he delivers the kingdom to God the Father . . . the Son himself will also be subjected to Him who put all things under him, that God may be everything to every one" (1 Cor. 15:24, 28).

Thus, perhaps the most important export that Americans and Westerners have yet to contribute to the building of world community is the knowledge that we are called by God as children of his covenant not to build a superchurch nor a supersynagogue but to search together for the true service to God's own people gathered from all the nations on the mountain of the Lord.

11.

Auschwitz and the Theology of the Holocaust

LIONEL RUBINOFF

It would be no exaggeration to claim that for the contemporary Jew, Auschwitz is the most decisive of all historical events. Like Nietzsche's death of God, "there never was a greater event" and "on account of it, all who are born after it belong to a different history." But unlike Nietzsche's event, which ushered in the possibility of a higher history for man, Auschwitz appears as the eclipse of history. Emil Fackenheim, with whose thought this essay will be chiefly concerned, reminds us in *Quest for Past and Future* that the essence of Judaism lies neither in an unchanging universality nor in the unique immediacy of the individual; it lies rather in an openness which listens and responds, works and waits, in a context defined by tradition. It is receptiveness to the uniqueness of revelation within the context of tradition which is the source of structure for Judaism.[1] Thus, if I understand Fackenheim correctly, that a Jew "listens" from within the context of an eighteenth century ghetto in Eastern Europe, or from within the context of a twentieth century post-Auschwitz world of suburban America, is the source of uniqueness. That he listens in his post-Auschwitz context as a descendant of those who have traveled the route to Auschwitz from Mount Sinai, is the source of tradition. The essence of Judaism thus emerges dialectically from the tension between immediacy and tradition: a resolution to be achieved in action as well as in thought.

But can all such tensions be so resolved? In any genuine resolution it must be possible to establish a measure of internal coherence. But what continuity, if any, can be found between the secular world of American Judaism and tradition, or between Auschwitz and tradition? In the course of confronting this challenge Fackenheim addresses himself to three specific questions: (1) Why a commitment to any religious truth? (2) Why

1. Emil Fackenheim, *Quest for Past and Future* (Boston: Beacon, 1968), pp. 3–26.

a commitment to Judaism? and (3) How respond Jewishly in the here and now? Or, to put it more specifically, How carry on the midrashim ("interpretation," "commentary") tradition into the twentieth century?

The gist of Fackenheim's response to the first two questions is that the very raising of the question is itself an event of Jewish significance. For whether the questioner is explicitly aware of it or not, he raises his questions as a Jew questioning the grounds of his Jewish commitment. Perhaps, then, these are questions for which there is no response except to recognize that the very raising of the question is itself an affirmation.

The third question is in many respects the most challenging. For, as Fackenheim puts it: the characteristic feature of the midrashim tradition, the tradition through which the Jew responds Jewishly to his here and now, is that Jewish thought, however firmly rooted in past revelatory events, has always remained open to present and future, and this openness includes vulnerability to radical surprise.

> The Torah was given at Sinai, yet it is given whenever a man receives it, and a man must often hear the old commandments in new ways. There are times in history when evil can be explained as deserved punishment, others when no such explanation is possible—when divine power is "as it were" suspended, and God himself suffers in exile. Such openness is necessary if history is to be serious.[2]

The test of this capacity for openness, according to Fackenheim, is nowhere greater than in the challenge of Auschwitz. Auschwitz is the scandal of evil for evil's sake and Jews were the singled out victims. The vulnerability to radical surprise which characterizes Jewish theology and Jewish existence lies precisely in the fact that it must be prepared to confront such events as Auschwitz. If I may generalize from this doctrine of Fackenheim's concerning the nature of Jewish theology in particular, I would suggest that, just as events like Auschwitz constitute the focal points of Jewish theology, so events like Hiroshima, My Lai, and the current ecological disasters which threaten to bring all human existence to an end before the end of the present century, constitute challenges for theology in general, Jewish and non-Jewish alike.

How can a Jew respond Jewishly to an event like Auschwitz? This response, according to Fackenheim, takes the form not only of memory but of witness. Not to remember would be blasphemy. Not to be a witness would be a betrayal. For a Jew, to respond through memory and

2. *Ibid.*, p. 17.

witness is to commit himself to survival as a Jew. To dedicate oneself as a Jew to survival in the age of Auschwitz is in itself a monumental act of faith. To be a Jew after Auschwitz is to confront the demons of Auschwitz and to bear witness against them in all their guises. It is to assert as the basis of one's beliefs the conviction that evil will not prevail and to stake one's life and those of one's children on this conviction. Indeed, as Fackenheim represents it, Auschwitz reexperienced is nothing short of revelation. Through that revelation of reliving Auschwitz the Jew is commanded to survive as a Jew through memory and witness in order that Hitler may not be permitted a posthumous victory. Jews are forbidden also to despair of God and of the world as the domain of God lest the world be handed over to the forces of Auschwitz. For a Jew to break this commandment would be to do the unthinkable—to respond to Hitler by doing his work.[3]

Fackenheim argues strenuously that whatever the response to Auschwitz, it must, following Jewish tradition, take the form of a stubborn persistence in our Jewishness, and not an attempt to abandon or escape from it. Although Fackenheim believes that the tradition of universal secular humanism, as represented, for example, by the writings of George Steiner, does not succeed in capturing either the paradox of God's presence in history or the essence of Auschwitz, he can at least respect it and enter into dialogue with it. He will not, however, attempt to dialogue with unauthentic Jews who use Auschwitz as an excuse for abandoning their commitments to Judaism. This does not mean that he expects authentic Jews to be totally unshaken in their faith. On the contrary, according to Fackenheim, the real test of faith in the post-Holocaust world comes only when the Jew risks self-exposure to both secularism and secular nihilism. Religious immediacy must expose itself both to the threat of the critical reflection of positivism (which reduces history to natural law and religious experience to psychology, thus dissipating God's historical presence in history) and historical nihilism, which uses Auschwitz as evidence of the futility of belief. For the authentic Jew, tradition and commitment can be affirmed only by stepping outside that tradition and commitment, thus calling it into question. Such a stance of faith was called by Kierkegaard "immediacy after reflection."

For Fackenheim the essence of immediacy after reflection is found in a remarkable passage from Martin Buber's *Moses*, a passage so

3. *Ibid.*, p. 20.

profound in its implications that it deserves to be cited in full. Speaking of events like the exodus, which form the core of the sacred history of Judaism, Buber writes:

> What is decisive with respect to the inner history of Mankind . . . is that the children of Israel understood this as an act of their God, as a "miracle"; which does not mean that they interpreted it as a miracle, but that they experienced it as such, that as such they perceived it. . . .
>
> The concept of miracle, which is permissible from the historical approach can be defined at its starting point as an abiding astonishment. The . . . religious person . . . abides in that wonder; no knowledge, no cognition, can weaken his astonishment. Any causal explanation only deepens the wonder for him. The great turning-points in religious history are based on the fact that again and ever again an individual and a group attached to him wonder and keep on wondering; at a natural phenomenon, at an historical event, or at both together; always at something which intervenes fatefully in the life of this individual and this group. They sense and experience it as a wonder. This, to be sure, is only the starting-point of the historical concept of wonder, but it cannot be explained away. Miracle is not something "supernatural" or "superhistorical," but an incident, an event which can be fully included in the objective, scientific nexus of nature and history; the vital meaning of which, however, for the person to whom it occurs, destroys the security of the whole nexus of knowledge for him, and explodes the fixity of the fields of experience named "Nature" and "History" . . .
>
> We may ascribe what gives rise to our astonishment to a specific power. . . . For the performance of the miracle a particular magical spirit, a special demon, a special idol is called into being. It is an idol just because it is special. But this is not what historical consideration means by miracle. For where a doer is restricted by other doers, the current system of cause and effect is replaced by another. . . . The real miracle means that in the astonishing experience of the event the current system of cause and effect becomes, as it were, transparent and permits a glimpse of the sphere in which a sole power, not restricted by any other, is at work.[4]

According to the dialectic implicit in Buber's version of "immediacy after reflection," the believer exposes his faith to criticism and this brings him into the midst of doubt and despair with respect to his formerly held beliefs. He then steps back once again and becomes critical of his criticism, with the result that he transcends immediacy only to be returned to his original beliefs transformed. The Jew having suffered the dialectic of criticism continues to participate in tradition and in the re-

4. Martin Buber, *Moses* (Oxford, London: East & West Library, n.d.), pp. 75–77.

covery of the primordial root experiences upon which Judaism is founded, but no longer in a religious immediacy which has never thought of stepping outside the traditional framework. Neither does he adopt a stance of pure critical reflection which stands outside only and merely looks on. Nothing is possible except an immediacy after reflection which is and remains self-exposed to the possibility of a total dissipation of every divine presence, and yet confronts this possibility with a forever reenacted risk of commitment.[5] Auschwitz no less than the logic of scientific-secular rationalism constitutes such a challenge to religious immediacy and every individual Jew is obliged, in his own way, to encounter this challenge.

For Fackenheim the tradition from which the Jew begins and to which he returns following his encounter with immediacy after reflection is the tradition of the Midrash. The midrashic tradition takes the form of a stubborn persistence of Jewishness and not an attempt to abandon it or escape from it.[6] The question to be faced is, How is it possible and indeed necessary for the Jew of today to be a witness to the world?[7] To this question the midrashic tradition provides at least the outline of an answer. And that answer takes the form of an affirmation of God's presence in history. But the ancient Midrash not only affirms God's presence in history, it suffers the contradictions inherent in that presence as well.

The essence of the midrashic tradition lies in the notion of what Fackenheim calls "the root experience," the direct experience of God's presence in history. Against the midrashic affirmation, however, modern man seems compelled to deny that presence. The study of nature reveals not God but blind natural laws, while the study of history reveals man at the mercy of his passions. God it seems must be expelled from history just as he is expelled from nature. The contemporary theologian would thus seem to have no option but to affirm at most the providence of God over nature and history, a providence caused by a God who may somehow use nature and man in history, but who is himself absent from history.

5. Emil Fackenheim, *God's Presence in History* (New York: New York University Press, 1970), p. 49.

6. *Ibid.*, p. 8; cf. also, Eli Weisel, "Jewish Values in the Post-Holocaust Future: A Symposium," *Judaism* 16 (Summer 1967): 269.

7. Fackenheim, *God's Presence in History*, p. 8, and *Quest for Past and Future*, p. 4.

Yet even this weakened doctrine is difficult to maintain. From the philosopher's point of view how can divine providence rule over history and yet allow human freedom within it? For the historian the question is, How can one believe in providential history in the face of evil? Finally, the scientist asks, How do we reconcile God's presence in nature in the face of the apparent indifference of nature to the affairs of men? Against these difficulties modern theologians have abandoned the stage-manager theory of God in favor of an immanentist's theory according to which either God's presence is itself the product of historical-human activity, so that his very being is synonymous with the progressive realization of human freedom, or else while God's being transcends history his presence can nevertheless be detected through the experience of a providence in the form of progress which is immanent in human freedom. According to the first model, meaning is both created in as well as realized through history, while according to the second model, meaning, although it pre-exists to history, is nevertheless progressively realized through history.

Traditional responses to the challenges of nature and history thus sought refuge in the doctrines of progress and the cunning of reason. St. Thomas, for example, argued that tyrants serve providential ends, for if it were not for tyrants there would be no opportunity for martyrdom. After Auschwitz such an argument is blasphemous if not obscene. Philosophers like Kant and Hegel seriously proposed that war served the purposes of providence. Hegel began his lectures on the philosophy of history with the recognition that history confronts us with a display of passion, violence, and evil.[8] At the same time, he argued, reason is the law of the world.[9] But it is an immanent principle of history which means that it can reach its own perfection only in and through *historical* existence,[10] that is to say, through the very display of evils to which our attention was originally drawn. Hegel thus affirms without qualification that nothing great in the world has been accomplished without passion[11] and we must therefore ask, when contemplating history as the slaughter-bench at which the happiness of peoples has been sacrificed, "To what principle, to what final purpose, have these monstrous sacrifices been offered?"[12] That principle is freedom, which is God's purpose with

8. G. W. F. Hegel, *Reason in History*, tr. R. S. Hartman (Indianapolis: Bobbs-Merrill Co., 1963), p. 26.
9. *Ibid.*, p. 11.
10. *Ibid.*, p. 31.
11. *Ibid.*, p. 29.
12. *Ibid.*, p. 27.

the world, a purpose to be inferred from the freedom actualized throughout history. To this end all the sacrifices have been offered on the vast altar of the earth throughout the long lapse of ages.[13] After Hiroshima and My Lai it is difficult if not perverse to support this view.

If anything, the spectacles of Hiroshima, Auschwitz, and My Lai seem to have destroyed any continuing belief in the providence of Hegel's immanent principle of reason, while the recent catastrophes of nature, such as famine, drought, earthquakes, and floods, fast remove any remaining confidence in the providential character of nature. After these dread events, how can one believe in any kind of God let alone a God of history?

It is clear that the trauma of contemporary events affects all religious belief, as well as all moral belief, and we are well on the way to affirming the loci of nihilism according to which, if nothing has any meaning and if we can affirm no values whatsoever, then everything is possible and nothing has any importance. Evil and virtue are mere chance or caprice. And since nothing is either true or false, good or bad, we are as free to stoke the crematory fires as to work for justice. Even a conventionalist like Hume or an intuitionist like G. E. Moore would have difficulty sustaining any continued confidence in the integrity of a moral universe. Indeed, the scandal of events like Hiroshima and Auschwitz lies in the fact that their legitimation, for those who condoned them, was believed to rest on a set of intuitively self-evident truths supported by the very same language which has supported the traditional morality of common sense. And this poses the decisive problem for Western culture and belief in general.

Emil Fackenheim, however, poses the problem for the Jew in particular. Indeed, he argues, it is Jewish belief which is the most traumatically affected. In the first place, the Jewish people were the first to affirm the God of history. They have had a unique relation to this God in the sense that in their case alone collective survival itself was bound up with him. In the second place the Jewish faith rests absolutely upon the reality of past experiences affirming God's actual presence in history. It would thus be a total contradiction of Jewish tradition to either turn away from God altogether or else seek God outside of history, whether in eternity, in nature, or in progress. It would be just as contradictory to turn even to an individualistic mystical inwardness. Traditional Jewish faith has not only refused to despair of God, it also refused to disconnect

13. *Ibid.*, p. 25.

him from history and to seek an escape in mysticism or otherworldliness.[14]

Is this merely the result of blind stubbornness, of a dogmatic refusal even to face up to the possibility of either alternate religious flights from history or else irreligious flights from Jewishness itself? Or can the midrashic tradition be authenticated in the context of what we have previously called "immediacy after reflection"?

To answer this question we must return once again to the notion of "the root experience." The root experience is essentially the direct experience of God's presence in history and is accompanied, on the side of the witness, by an experience of "abiding astonishment." There are at least two primary forms of root experiences which Fackenheim distinguishes as the experience of "saving presence" in which God is experienced as "sole power" and the experience of "commanding voice." The divine presence is thus synonymous with the experience of "saving presence" and "commanding voice." The parting of the Red Sea is the prototype of saving presence while the events at Sinai constitute a commanding presence. But even in saving presence there is commanding presence, for at the Red Sea no salvation would have occurred had Israel shrunk in fear from walking through the divided sea. Thus a commanding voice is heard even as the saving event is seen and salvation is not complete until the voice is heeded.

Such a presence is, in the first instance, nothing short of paradoxical. As "sole power" in the form of "saving presence" God's presence would appear to be an acknowledgment of the limitation of human freedom; one might even regard it as a negation of that freedom. At the same time, as commanding presence, God is experienced as addressing human freedom. Thus the freedom which is suspended by "sole power" is required by commanding presence.

In the face of this paradox midrashic tradition makes the following response. The divine commanding presence can be divine, commanding, and present only if it is doubly present, as both the affirmation and the negation of human freedom. And this means that the human astonishment which accompanies the experience of that presence must be a double astonishment, the astonishment of man who experiences himself as both free and yet limited: a feeling which parallels the equally astonishing experience of being between revelation and redemption, of suffering the experience that man is not—and the faith that he will be—what

14. Fackenheim, *God's Presence in History*, p. 7.

God means him ultimately to be. As sole power, the divine commanding presence destroys human freedom; as gracious power, it not only restores but exalts that freedom. Indeed, human freedom is made a part of the covenant with divinity itself. And the human astonishment which is terror at a presence at once divine and commanding, turns into a second astonishment, which is joy, at a grace which restores and exalts human freedom by its commanding presence.

According to the Midrash, all generations of Israel were present at Sinai and the Torah is therefore given whenever a man receives it, regardless of time or place in history. Each historical generation thus earns its heritage by reenacting for itself, through both memory and deed, the reception of the Torah. Root experiences are events which are logically different from ordinary historical events. For whereas the latter are such that it is sometimes possible to achieve a definitive understanding sufficient to warrant, as it were, "closing the file," the root experience is by definition incapable of being so recorded. Root experiences cannot therefore be forgotten. Indeed, the very being of the root experience is to be remembered, and in each recovery of that memory is added a fresh immediacy, a new form of uniqueness. And this means reenacting the experience as paradox and therefore suffering the experience as double astonishment. If in the reenactment of that experience the individual Jew remains frozen in stark terror, he cannot observe the commandments; and if he evades that terror, he may observe the commandments but he has lost the divine commanding presence. Only by reenacting both the terror and the joy can he participate in a life of the commandments which lives before the sole power and yet is human.

In this response midrashic reflection shows itself to be aware of the all-pervasive dialectical contradictions which derive from the divine presence, the contradictions between divine transcendence and divine involvement and between divine power and human freedom. But unlike philosophy which, in its effort to elevate itself to the rank of a science, seeks to resolve all such contradictions to the satisfaction of thought, midrashic reflection resists the temptation to resolve contradictions. Indeed, Fackenheim argues, midrashic thinking refuses *a priori* to destroy these experiences even though it is prepared to stand outside and reflect upon them, thus disclosing to itself the inherent contradictions. For midrashic thought cannot resolve the contradictions in the root experiences of Judaism but can only seek to express them.[15]

15. *Ibid.*, p. 20.

This, if I understand Fackenheim correctly, is no mere triviality. For to express and suffer the anguish of a contradiction which reason discloses but which neither reason nor faith can resolve is to approach the boundaries of mystery with a fear and trembling sufficient to shake a man's being at the very root of its foundations. There is all the difference in the world between the abiding astonishment accompanying the immediacy which precedes the reflection, and the abiding astonishment which survives and accompanies the celebration of mystery which is immediacy after reflection. Likewise there is a profound difference in the very quality of a man's being who has undergone such an experience.

Just as midrashic thought confronts the challenge of the very *a priori* of God's presence in history, so does it respond to the challenges of science, scientism, and history itself, including the history of evil and catastrophe.

But as we have already acknowledged, the greatest challenge to midrashic thought is the Holocaust whose symbol is Auschwitz. It is difficult enough to comprehend the possibility of a midrashic encounter with the ordinary history of evil. It is utterly incomprehensible how there could be immediacy after reflection on Auschwitz; incomprehensible that is, unless we are to regard Auschwitz not simply as a challenge to the root experience but as itself a root experience. But this is precisely what Fackenheim proposes. Following Elie Weisel's suggestion that the Holocaust may be compared with Sinai as revelatory significance, Fackenheim, with a boldness and daring unparalleled, I suggest, in the history of recent theology, turns his ear to the Holocaust and listens. And what he hears, through the reenactment of that root experience in accordance with midrashic tradition, is what he refers to as "the commanding voice of Auschwitz." Thus is revealed the six-hundred-fourteenth commandment, according to which the authentic Jew of today is forbidden to hand Hitler yet another posthumous victory.

> Jews are forbidden to hand Hitler posthumous victories. They are commanded to survive as Jews, lest the Jewish people perish. They are commanded to remember the victims of Auschwitz lest their memory perish. They are forbidden to despair of man and his world, and to escape into either cynicism or otherworldliness, lest they cooperate in delivering the world over to the forces of Auschwitz. Finally, they are forbidden to despair of the God of Israel, lest Judaism perish. A secularist Jew cannot make himself believe by a mere act of will, nor can he be commanded to do so. . . . And a religious Jew who has stayed

> with God his God may be forced into new, possibly revolutionary relationships with Him. One possibility, however, is wholly unthinkable. A Jew may not respond to Hitler's attempt to destroy Judaism by himself cooperating in its destruction.[16]

But how is such a commandment to be obeyed in a post-Auschwitz world? If the double astonishment which accompanies the revelation of Sinai is difficult to bear, what can be said of the astonishment which accompanies the revelation of Auschwitz? The astonishment is made all the deeper by the fact that whereas at Sinai the Jew hears the commanding voice of a God who is present, at Auschwitz he hears a commanding voice at the same time that he experiences the absence of God. The commanding voice of Auschwitz is the voice of a God in exile. Is such a notion merely the result of madness, the madness of a midrashic tradition tortured by paradox after paradox until it finally breaks down altogether? Is this perhaps the real legacy of Auschwitz, that in their attempt to preserve the authenticity of midrashic tradition the best minds of our generation have been destroyed by madness?

Perhaps it is a madness of a sort, to think this way, and to suggest the possibility that even in Auschwitz there is revelation. But if so, perhaps it is a madness without which man cannot be man. Perhaps never before has man been so much of a man than when he humbles himself before the commanding voice of Auschwitz—for by heeding that commandment, in the only way it can be heeded, with imagination and courage and creativity, we Jews who come after not only preserve the memory of the dead, and honor the presence of those who survived, but we dignify and consecrate that death in the most sublime manner possible, by providing future generations with abiding astonishment at the manner in which we have listened to and have heeded that commandment. For what is affirmed through the memory of Auschwitz is not the demonic madness which produced it, but the divine madness of our response to it.

Whenever one attempts to meditate along such difficult lines one is always tempted to seek out analogues. In this connection I cannot help thinking of a story by Philip Roth which has always haunted my critical imagination and which in its own way expresses the madness of midrashic stubbornness in the face of absurdity. It is the story called "Eli the Fanatic."

16. *Ibid.*, p. 84; cf. also Weisel, "Jewish Values," pp. 272–3; Emil Fackenheim, "Jewish Faith and the Holocaust," *Commentary* 46 (August 1968):30–36.

The story, if you remember, concerns the middle class community of Woodenton, typical of so many American suburbs, and outstanding for the fact that Jews and gentiles live side by side in harmonious togetherness. But the day arrives when the Jewish community is threatened by the specter of its past—symbolized by the opening of a yeshiva for displaced children whose parents had died in Hitler's gas chambers. The most disturbing spectacle of all is the sight of a bearded Hasidic Jew, dressed in a black suit and wearing a black hat, walking down the main streets of Woodenton. The more responsible members of the community, who regard themselves as the vanguard of the new American assimilated Jew, engage a lawyer, Eli Peck, and instruct him to secure the immediate and total removal of the yeshiva, and especially of the man with the hat. The hat and the suit soon become the symbol of the whole problem. Among the complaints, the following seem particularly crucial: "Someday," warns Harry Shaw, "it's going to be a hundred little kids with little *yarmulkehs* chanting their Hebrew lessons on Coach House Road . . . "; "Goddam fanatics," exclaims another irrate member of the community, "This is the twentieth century. Now its the guy with the hat. Pretty soon all the little Yeshiva boys'll be spilling down into town. Next thing they'll be after our daughters." And finally, Eli Peck says to himself, as he tries to make sense of the whole business, "If that guy would take off that crazy hat . . . I know it's what eats them. If he'd just take off that crazy hat everything would be all right."[17]

Eli tries to persuade the yeshiva to relocate, but without success. When it becomes clear that the yeshiva cannot be moved (a symbol of the historic fact that the Jews have refused to be exterminated) the officials decide to be "tolerant" and "liberal" and they extend an invitation to the director of the yeshiva to assimilate. The conditions under which their continued presence will be tolerated are stated in a letter which Eli presents, on behalf of the assimilated community of Woodenton, to Mr. Tzuref, the director of the yeshiva. The letter reads as follows:

> Dear Mr. Tzuref:
>
> Our meeting this evening seems to me inconclusive. I don't think there's any reason for us not to be able to come up with some sort of compromise that will satisfy the Jewish community of Woodenton and the Yeshivah and yourself. It seems to me that what most disturbs my neighbors are the visits to town by the gentleman in the black hat, suit,

17. Philip Roth, *Goodbye Columbus* (Boston: Houghton Mifflin Company, 1959), pp. 187–90.

etc. Woodenton is a progressive suburban community whose members, both Jewish and Gentile, are anxious that their families live in comfort and beauty and serenity. This is, after all, the 20th century, and we do not think it too much to ask that the members of our community dress in a manner appropriate to the time and place.

Woodenton, as you may not know, has long been the home of well-to-do Protestants. It is only since the war that Jews have been able to buy property here, and for Jews and Gentiles to live beside each other in amity. For this adjustment to be made, both Jews and Gentiles alike have had to give up some of their more extreme practices in order not to threaten or offend the other. Certainly such amity is to be desired. Perhaps if such conditions had existed in pre-war Europe, the persecution of the Jewish people, of which you and those 18 children have been victims, could not have been carried out with such success—in fact, might not have been carried out at all.

Therefore, Mr. Tzuref, will you accept the following conditions. If you can, we will see fit not to carry out legal action against the Yeshivah for failure to comply with township zoning ordinances Nos. 18 and 23. The conditions are simply:

1. The religious, educational, and social activities of the Yeshivah of Woodenton will be confined to the Yeshivah grounds.
2. Yeshivah personnel are welcomed in the streets and stores of Woodenton provided they are attired in clothing usually associated with American life in the 20th century.

If these conditions are met, we see no reason why the Yeshivah of Woodenton cannot live peacefully and satisfactorily with the Jews of Woodenton—as the Jews of Woodenton have come to live with the Gentiles of Woodenton. I would appreciate an immediate reply.

Sincerely,
Mr. Peck, Attorney

Two days after delivering his letter Eli received his reply, in one sentence, which in my opinion sums up the whole essence of the matter, and speaks for itself without need of further comment.

Dear Mr. Peck:

The suit the gentleman wears is all he's got.

Sincerely,
Leo Tzuref[18]

Fackenheim's six-hundred-fourteenth commandment is in keeping with the traditional midrashic obligation to survive as a Jew in order that the messianic promise of God to man will be fulfilled. It is also in keeping with the demands of tradition to survive as a Jew by reenacting the

18. *Ibid.*

root experiences of Judaism in the context of the Jew's contemporary situation—which in our case is a post-Auschwitz world. It is also in keeping with the messianic obligation to survive through creativity. The essence of this dimension of messianism is contained, I suggest, in a remark of Martin Buber's about the teachings of the Ba'al Shem Tov, the founder of Hasidism. The Ba'al Shem Tov, according to Buber, explained the meaning of man's being created in the image of God, this way: "The man of true piety takes unto himself the quality of fervour, for he is hallowed and become like the Holy one, blessed be He, when He created His world."[19] Responding to this passage, Buber writes: "It was then that I experienced the Hasidic soul. The primarily Jewish opened to me, flowering to newly conscious expression in the darkness of exile: man's being created in the image of God I grasped as deed, as becoming, as task. And primarily Jewish reality was a primal human reality: the content of human religiousness opened to me there."[20]

From Hasidism, then, Buber learned to find the essence of religion in creativity. As God made man, so man must remake the world as well as himself. The essence of piety is creativity, not simply passive submission to inevitability. Nor does creativity mean secular success. This creativity embraces the two central areas of Jewish concern, which are man's duties to God and man's duties to himself. Only from these two expressions of love can despair be transcended.

Following the spirit inherent in the Ba'al Shem Tov's affirmation of Judaism, Fackenheim's six-hundred-fourteenth commandment can be restated as follows. Auschwitz was an attempt to exterminate Jews. As such it was the symbol of destruction, the end of creation. It was also a glorification of satanic intoxication with power and technology, of the pornographic exercise of power. Therefore midrashic stubbornness commands not only survival, but survival through creativity and love, and survival by means of the logic of justice rather than of power and domination. Even though all the forces of technology and power were turned against them, Jews have shown themselves to be greater than the forces which sought to destroy them because they comprehend the advantage that power has over innocence. To so realize the finitude of man is a cause for despair. Yet amidst that despair there is joy, the joy of realizing that in spite of the advantage which the forces of demonic evil have

19. Martin Buber, *Hasidism and Modern Man* (New York: Harper Torchbook, 1966), p. 185.

20. *Ibid.*

over innocence—and what more vivid affirmation of the pathos of this condition can be cited than the original myth—man yet has the freedom to create. That freedom to create expresses itself on the one hand through the collective sharing of memory and through "caring" as opposed to domination. If the post-Auschwitz world is now characterized by a domination of Faust over Prometheus then Jews are dedicated to the restoration of the rationality of "caring," of listening with the heart, as Buber puts it. The true language of celebration, in response to openness to being, is not the kind of calculative cleverness that expresses itself in fascination for "technique," "final solutions," "organization of means to realize goals regardless of consequences," but "*mitzvah*" and "*simchath*."

But simply to contrast mitzvah in the form of caring with the mechanistic, functional rationality of *l'homme machine* is not enough. Nor is it enough to simply "care" and be "cared for." For the fact is that such caring is not possible in a world dominated by the logic of *l'homme machine*. To confront and respond to Auschwitz is thus to confront and respond to the corrupt rationality which it symbolizes and which still infects every aspect of our culture. To confront Auschwitz thus means not only to listen to the six-hundred-fourteenth commandment in the midst of abiding astonishment, which is the source of its uniqueness as an event in Jewish history, but to confront the inherent crisis of rationality which is the source of its universality. Midrashic stubbornness begins with a refusal to be terrorized by Auschwitz into adopting a posture of apocalyptic despair and includes a refusal to be dominated by the inherent irrationality brought about by the logic of domination.

But this protest must begin with diagnosis. The Jewish response to Auschwitz is not only affirmation of messianic faith but social diagnosis. What is the nature of man and society that events like Auschwitz are possible. I don't mean by this that we should adopt the style of the social sciences which try to grasp the particular in terms of universals. I am suggesting not a covering-law explanation leading to *erklären* but historical understanding leading to *verstehen* which proceeds from particular to universal.

I am thus advocating, in addition to Fackenheim's midrashic response, the need for a phenomenology of contemporary Jewish existence in the light of a hermeneutic derived from midrashic tradition. The contemporary authentic Jew speaks of God through the celebration of an existence which refuses to allow itself to be determined by an essence dictated by

Auschwitz, and refuses therefore to conform either to the logic of domination or the logic of nihilism. According to the logic of the Midrash, as represented by Fackenheim, a God who is present in history must be present differently than if he were present in the form of pure transcendence. To be present historically means to be subject to the conditions of historicity. This means that God manifests himself differently according to the exigencies of the historical moment. This is the ground of pluralism and thus commands respect for pluralism. At the same time it opens the danger of relativism, in the form of an idolatrous pluralism of sheer diversity without unity, which paradoxically dissipates respect. For to respect all appearances equally is equivalent to the belief in nothing, with which the logic of nihilism begins and which in turn concludes with the logic of power. In order to assault from the outset this temptation to believe in the many gods of idolatrous pluralism, the Midrash teaches that while a God manifest in history manifests himself differently—as mighty hero doing battle as in the case of the Red Sea, as old man full of mercy as at Sinai—he is nevertheless manifest in each moment as the one sole power of every moment. But, and this is the crucial insight asserted by midrashic logic, the universality of the sole power manifested in a unique saving event demands a correspondingly universal human recognition of its universality, thus inspiring the poetic truth of the universal abolition of pluralism in the form of idolatry. And so it is said, "Who is like unto thee, O Lord, among the mighty?"[21] The social diagnosis of the post-Auschwitz Jew is dedicated to expose the pathology of idolatrous pluralism and to reaffirm the unity of truth as midrashic tradition reaffirms the unity of God.

Fackenheim points out that when taken as a whole the midrashic interpretation exposes serious contradictions. The first contradiction is suggested by the fact that a God who, by himself, was, is, and shall be, must yet be present differently if his presence is to be within history. What is more, the God who is Lord of history was, is, and shall be sovereign as sole power. Yet even in a supreme (albeit premessianic) manifestation of his power, he stands in need of human glorification; and the fact that this glorification is momentarily given by all the nations reveals more poignantly the paradox of a subsequent relapse into pluralistic idolatry by all nations, Israel herself included. Confronting this contradiction and commenting upon the verse, "This is my God and I will glorify

21. Exod. 15:11. Cf. also "Melrilta de-Rabbi Ishmael," in *Rabbinic Essays*, ed. J. Z. Lauterbach (New York: Ktav Publishing Company, 1951), 2:24 ff.

Him,"[22] Rabbi Yishmael asks: "Is it possible for a man of flesh and blood to add to the glory of his creator?"[23] For *a parte subjecti* unless divine presence requires human recognition man loses all significance and his obedience would seem at best purely abstract, while *a parte objecti,* the power of the divine would seem to depend upon God's transcendence—a condition which does not coincide with traditional belief in divine historical presence.

On the other hand, if human glorification and recognition is required, then even a saving presence, not to speak of a commanding presence, is incomplete without it. The question thus persists: How can human praise and recognition add to the divine glory and yet human failure to give praise not diminish it? Or, How can human failure weaken the power on high? "Ye are my witnesses, saith the Lord . . . [and] I am the Lord."[24] According to midrashic tradition this may be interpreted as meaning: "When ye are my witnesses, I am God, and when ye are not my witnesses, I am, as it were, not God." Or, "When the Israelites do God's will, they add to the power of God on high. When the Israelites do not do God's will, they, as it were, weaken the great power of God."

But once again the question arises, How is human recognition and the freedom thus presupposed to be reconciled with divine power which is affirmed through recognition? As we have already noted, a saving presence requires recognition for a divine act which conceivably if only momentarily overwhelms human freedom. The paradox is that to affirm the glory of God in this context which *a parte subjecti* presupposes freedom is, insofar as what is confirmed implies, to affirm human powerlessness. At the same time, the commanding presence affirmed requires not simply recognition but *action,* in which case rather than freedom being overwhelmed by divine presence it must be affirmed. And what is affirmed is thus not simply the freedom to affirm but the freedom and indeed necessity to act. This is how it is both possible and necessary for the Jew to be a witness to the world and why it is necessary, to return to Philip Roth's story, for the Jew not to take off the black hat.

Thus it seems that the paradox of God's presence in history is that he is both sole power and yet dependent upon human recognition, that he both acknowledges man's powerlessness yet affirms human freedom. Fackenheim argues that the contradictions between divine transcendence

22. Exod. 15:2.
23. "Melrilta de-Rabbi Ishmael," 2:25.
24. Isa. 43:10–12.

and divine involvement and between divine power and human freedom are not resolved, but only expressed. What is clear, however, is that unless obedience and disobedience, recognition or nonrecognition, man's exercise or escape from freedom, made a difference, divinity could not be historically present as commanding, and unless there was at least some perceptual evidence of salvation, God could not be present as saving. It may not be possible to *account* for these conditions. Yet they must be presupposed. And because they remain unresolved there is the need for a final consummation in the future in the form of a messianic age which can only be achieved by listening to and accepting the injunction of the commanding voice of Auschwitz, and by accepting it in the context of the obligation to perform not only the mitzvahs commanded by divine law, but the social diagnosis which alone makes possible the performance of those mitzvahs through which the messianic promise will be realized. For this reason, as Fackenheim has insisted, Jews must remember Auschwitz and be its witness to the world. Not to remember would be blasphemy. Not to be a witness would be a betrayal.[25]

Just as midrashic stubbornness commands recognition of divine presence in spite of the fragmentariness of theological speculation, so Jewish social and personal existence is commanded to live by trust, rather than mere argument. Because the universe is silent with respect to the resolution of paradox and mystery is no excuse for skeptical paralysis or cynical nihilism. Jewish existence commands an affirmation of values in the midst of tension and despair. What is important, however, is that we continue to exist without illusions. To say, in accordance with midrashic logic, that God's power is diminished by human failure to respond through "caring" is to emphasize the importance of not confusing man's witness through creativity with progress or even "culture" in the sense of technique. When George Steiner, for example, confronts Auschwitz as the failure of culture, his reflection parallels the Jewish theologians' confrontation of the absence of God in Auschwitz. Like the theologian, Steiner focuses attention on the fundamental *hybris* of Western man's idolatry of identifying God's presence as power, technology, technique, and mastery: the very faustian, satanic temptations prefigured in the myth. And like the Jewish theologian, Steiner too emerges from his encounter with Auschwitz only to reaffirm in his "immediacy after reflection" the fundamental values of humanity so utterly violated by the horrors of Auschwitz. What we are asked to remember, then, through

25. Fackenheim, *Quest for Past and Future*, p. 18.

the memory of Auschwitz, are not just the idols of culture who decreed it, but the Jewish soul, as expressed in creativity and caring, whether in life or death. And when we remember the victims of Auschwitz we pay tribute not to the glory of man's temple or worldly achievements but to the human capacity to grow through caring.

Any meditation upon Auschwitz must be undertaken in a mood of humility as well as solemnity. I frankly doubt whether the rules normally associated with the tradition of academic disputation apply to discussions of Auschwitz. Just as Auschwitz is itself an episode in the history of obscenity, so the attempt to debate and dispute its significance risks becoming an expression of academic pornography. One cannot debate Auschwitz in the manner in which philosophers are accustomed to debate whether there are synthetic *a priori* truths, or whether it is possible to argue from the "is" to the "ought." The truth about Auschwitz is not a prize to be competed for. The radical uniqueness of Auschwitz lies as much in its refusal to be comprehended in terms of the normal categories of scientific inquiry as in its effects on the lives of its victims. Perhaps all that can be said is that each man suffers the event for himself and that rather than pretending to announce the truth in the sense that scientists pretend to give us explanations and theories, the historian of Auschwitz can only express, through the telling of the tale, the truth of his own unique encounter, a uniqueness which gives rise to universality only when it is responded to through affirmation. I do not know what it would mean to respond in turn to such affirmations except through a similar affirmation, which then becomes the basis of sharing.

But how does one share the uniqueness of an encounter with radical uniqueness? The radical uniqueness of Auschwitz lies in its radical absurdity, in the fact that it is pure, demonic evil, evil for evil's sake. This was not evil committed, as it so often is, for the sake of power, wealth, pleasure, self-interest, or even revenge. The structure of evil at Auschwitz thus appears to defy comprehension through the mediation of any kind of rationale. To face such evil and respond to it is therefore the greatest test the Jew has ever had to endure. In the case of all other evils that have been visited upon the Jewish people throughout their history there had at least been a reason and an explanation. And it was therefore both possible and reasonable to believe that once the conditions which nourished these reasons were eliminated then evil would disappear as well. But such hopes fled together with faith up the chimneys of Auschwitz.

Faced with the absurdity of Auschwitz, can we expect our response to it to be any less absurd? Some have responded by arguing that after Auschwitz either Jews should give up their Jewishness or else should no longer have children. But this is an unauthentic response because it involves total betrayal not only of Auschwitz but of Jewish tradition. Yet after Auschwitz such a judgment no matter how justified must be made with compassion. Others respond by telling us that the best we can do is continue to remember and tell the tale. But consider how poor and inadequate is the language of man when confronted by the terror of Auschwitz! We remember, yet we cannot speak. Perhaps, then, the only authentic language of that memory is silence. As the Kotzker Rebbe once said: The oral Torah tradition that we know is not the real one; the true Torah *she-bal peh* remained oral and secret.[26]

Yet even silence is being. Confronted by the poverty of language, man sees that language can no longer become a substitute for action. Instead of seeking evidence of the divine presence in explanations and theodicies, consciousness now experiences the silent power of the divine presence through action. The Jewish response to Holocaust thus takes the form of action, both the universal action of love, charity, piety, and creativity, as well as the uniquely Jewish action of stubborn midrashic commitment to remaining Jewish. Through such actions we Jews can respond with a more radical *af al pi chen* than Jews have ever had to show in their history. But it must be *as Jews* that we act, as Jews who remember Auschwitz, not simply as mankind-in-general. There is all the difference in the world between the love of man-in-general and the love of a Jew whose Jewishness has been nourished in the memory of Auschwitz. For when I reach out my hand to my fellow man, in love and in trust, it is the hand of a man who still bears the charred memory of Auschwitz in his bones. If I respond to Auschwitz through affirmation of my Jewishness then my response can in turn be responded to; that is to say, shared, either directly by other Jews who respond in kind with personal affirmation, or else by non-Jews who respond by affirming the Jew's right to survive as a Jew so that the messianic promise can be fulfilled. Each, in its own way, is absurd. For a Jew it means to respond in the shadow of a God who, although absent, yet commands. The essence of such response is trust. For the Christian and non-Jew it is absurd because he must affirm uniqueness in which he cannot directly share. The essence of this response is also trust.

26. Weisel, "Jewish Values," p. 284.

But while we might agree that the uniqueness of Auschwitz lies beyond rational comprehension and that nothing less will do than to respond to a commanding voice that speaks from Auschwitz, we might also agree that there is a universal essence to Auschwitz, the importance of which can be neither ignored altogether nor minimized. There is universality in several senses. There is universality in the sense that it demonstrates that culture and cold-blooded murder do not necessarily exclude each other. It demonstrates also that culture and indifference to the spectacle of evil do not exclude each other. For Auschwitz carried out what the world by and large was prepared to see carried out. The Jew was the victim not only of demonic evil but of the indifference of mankind to what was happening. God's failure was matched by man's. And, as George Steiner charges, "Men are always accomplices to whatever leaves them indifferent."[27]

There is universality then in the responses that all men must make. For Germans, Auschwitz requires a ruthless examination of their whole history. For Christians, it provokes the need for a pitiless reckoning with the history of Christian anti-Semitism, and for confronting the kind of reasons that led a leading theologian to declare during the rise of Nazi terror: "The Church of Christ has never lost sight of the thought that 'the chosen people,' who nailed the redeemer of the world to the cross, must bear the curse for its action through a long history of suffering."[28] And finally, for the whole world Auschwitz demands an inquiry into the grounds of its indifference for twelve long years.

Such inquiries should not be confused with theories of suffering-in-general or persecution-in-general, which only permit the real issues to be evaded. For as we have already seen, Auschwitz is the rock on which throughout eternity all rational explanations will eventually be shipwrecked and break apart. Such investigations, if they are to be meaningful at all, must take the form of self-interrogation leading to affirmation. In the case of such interrogations there are no distinctions between fact and value or between the "is" and the "ought." To establish the facts is equivalent to knowing what ought to be. If the Jews at Auschwitz were victims of my indifference, then to accept that diagnosis is equivalent to both condemning continued indifference to evil on my part and to affirming the values of the victims of Auschwitz, which means assuming the obligation to bear witness to that event everafter. To recognize and

27. *Ibid.*, p. 278.
28. Dietrich Bonhoeffer, cited by Fackenheim in "Jewish Faith," p. 34.

accept the extent of one's own complicity in the drama of evil that was Auschwitz is to undergo substantial, not merely accidental, personal change and to act in a manner commensurate with that change. The inquiry into Auschwitz which it is the universal obligation of mankind to undertake, cannot be like the sign post which, although it may correctly point in the right direction, is itself under no obligation to actually go in the direction in which it points.

Resisting rational explanations, Auschwitz will forever resist religious explanations as well. In particular the attempt to find a purpose in Auschwitz is foredoomed to a total failure. Some have sought refuge in the ancient "for our sins we are punished." But it does not require much sophistication to rule this out as totally unacceptable. Secular Jews might even connect the Holocaust with the rise of the state of Israel. But while there is undoubtedly a causal connection here, to translate this into a purpose is intolerable and would constitute a vicious example of the fallacy *post hoc ergo propter hoc* ("after this, therefore because of this"). Equally intolerable would be any attempt to justify Israel on the grounds that it is the answer to the Holocaust. To so link these events together is to diminish them both. If Israel is a free and independent state it is not because of the Holocaust, although it may be out of respect for the Holocaust that Israel assumes its determination to maintain its messianic pledge. Thus we must agree with Fackenheim when he insists that "a total and uncompromising sweep must be made of these and other explanations, all designed to give purpose to Auschwitz. No purpose, religious or otherwise non-religious, will ever be found in Auschwitz. The very attempt to find one is blasphemous."[29]

Fackenheim distinguishes, and we have attempted to follow suit, between an attempt to seek explanation and a response. But, he points out, there is no precedent for such a response either in Jewish or non-Jewish history. Jewish faith finds no refuge in midrashim of divine powerlessness, none in otherworldliness, none in the redeeming power of martyrdom, and most of all, none in the view that Auschwitz is punishment for the sins of Israel. This is what makes Jewish existence today unique, without support from analogues anywhere in the past. This is the scandal of Auschwitz which, once confronted by Jewish faith, threatens total despair.[30]

29. Fackenheim, "Jewish Faith," p. 31.
30. Fackenheim, "Jewish Faith," p. 32, and *God's Presence in History*, p. 79.

But however we come to characterize the failure of a theology of Auschwitz, one thing is certain with respect to the theology of response. Does it not follow, after Auschwitz, that any Jewish willingness to suffer martyrdom will constitute an encouragement to potential criminals? After Auschwitz, is not even the saintliest Jew driven to the inexorable conclusion that—ironical as it may seem—he owes a moral obligation to the anti-Semites of the world not to encourage them by his own powerlessness? After Auschwitz Jews no longer seek to sanctify God by submitting themselves to death. There is no revelation in Auschwitz in the sense of purpose, but there is nonetheless revelation in the form of a commanding voice. The Jew is commanded to survive as Jew. And whereas survival might once have been regarded as without meaning, in the age of Auschwitz a Jewish commitment to survival is in itself a monumental act of faithfulness, as well as a monumental, albeit fragmentary, act of faith. Emil Fackenheim writes:

> Even to do no more than remain a Jew after Auschwitz is to confront the demons of Auschwitz in all their guises, and to bear witness against them. It is to believe that these demons cannot, will not, and must not prevail, and to stake on that belief one's own life and the lives of one's children, and of one's children's children. To be a Jew after Auschwitz is to have wrested hope for the Jew and for the world—from the abyss of total despair. In the words of a speaker at a recent gathering of Bergen-Belsen survivors, the Jew after Auschwitz has a second Shema Yisrael: no second Auschwitz, no second Bergen-Belsen, no second Buchenwald—anywhere in the world, for anyone in the world.[31]

The commanding voice at Auschwitz thus decrees that a Jew may not respond to Hitler's attempt to destroy Judaism totally by himself cooperating in that destruction. In ancient times, the unthinkable Jewish sin was idolatry. Today, it is to respond to Hitler by doing his work. To this idolatry the post-Auschwitz Jew responds by reaffirming that ancient tradition whereby Jews bind themselves to each other and to the past through the rituals of commemoration. Foremost among those rituals is the Yizkor (service for the dead) and to be a Jew is thus to be part of a community woven by memory—the memory whose knots are tied up by Yizkor, by the continuity that is summed up in the holy words: *Yiskor Elohim nishman aboh mori*—may God remember the name of . . .

31. Fackenheim, "Jewish Faith," p. 32.

12.

Speaking of God after Auschwitz

FRANKLIN SHERMAN

The fact that we are able to take up a topic such as "speaking of God after Auschwitz" indicates that a certain stage of maturity has been reached in Lutheran-Jewish conversations. It was not very long ago, after all, that doubt was widely expressed as to whether the deep issues of faith could be dealt with at all within such an interreligious setting. Were not these matters too personal, too particular, too burdened with the baggage of our respective histories to be the appropriate subject of a dialogue that envisioned a fresh start in our relations with one another?

It is to the credit of the planners of the Lutheran-Jewish conversations that from the start, they were bold enough to plunge into biblical and theological topics on which the deepest convictions of both sides could come to expression. Many of these topics, however, were ones on which there was so definite a body of conviction on both sides, worked out through centuries and even millenia of discussion, that the spokesmen for the two faith communities could to a large extent serve simply as reporters of the received doctrine on the matter. Perhaps this has been more true for Lutheranism, which has been much more ready to encapsulate its faith in doctrinal or dogmatic form than has Judaism. But with a topic such as the present one we confront a question to which there are no ready-made answers.

Even for Judaism, which has lived now with the memory of the Holocaust for a generation, it can hardly be said that there is a consensus as to its meaning—if the term "meaning" can be applied to so irrational and so tragic an event. Among Lutherans, at least American Lutherans, it is doubtful if the question has even been faced in a serious way. Thus its appearance on our agenda here should not be taken as an indication that the time is ripe for a final word to be spoken, but on the contrary, that the time is at hand for a real engagement with the problem to begin.

The present paper, therefore, has the character of an essay—being an effort to open up the question, rather than a definitive statement.

Our topic would be easier to deal with if it read, "Speaking of Man after Auschwitz." For I think it is rather clear what must be said about man after the experience of the Holocaust. Let me put it in terms of the thought of one of the lesser figures of the Lutheran Reformation, one Matthias Flacius Illyricus.

Both Lutheran and Calvinistic theology of the sixteenth century, as is well known, held to a very realistic, not to say pessimistic, doctrine of man. But Flacius pushed this anthropological realism too far. Sin, he said, has become man's very nature and substance, and the image of God in man has become the image of Satan. For this he was condemned by the Lutheran fathers, as may be seen in the First Article of the Formula of Concord of 1577; and this rejection was highly significant in preserving for Lutheranism a higher estimate of man's cultural and historical possibilities than it has sometimes been credited with. (One thinks here particularly of Reinhold Niebuhr's critique of what he calls the "cultural defeatism" of Lutheranism.)

But from the perspective of this age "after Auschwitz" we may have to say that Flacius simply was a man in advance of his time. When he said that the image of God in man had become the image of Satan, he was wrong in applying this to the whole human race. But he had what now must be considered a correct prevision of the depths to which man would fall in the persons of the mass murderers of our own age.

Listen to these words of Elie Weisel, in which he describes this phenomenon:

> It is possible to be born into the upper or middle-class, receive a first-rate education, respect parents and neighbors, visit museums and attend literary gatherings, play a role in public life, and begin one day to massacre men, women, and children, without hesitation and without guilt. It is possible to fire your gun at living targets and nonetheless delight in the cadence of a poem, the composition of a painting. One's spiritual legacy provides no screen, ethical concepts offer no protection. One may torture the son before his father's eyes and still consider oneself a man of culture and religion. And dream of a peaceful sunset over the sea.[1]

1. Elie Weisel, *One Generation After,* tr. Lily Edelman and the author (New York: Avon Books, 1972), p. 10. Copyright © 1970 by Random House, Inc. Reprinted by permission.

That is Satan garbed as an angel of light. And as the reports of the Vietnam atrocities have shown, it is not only in Germany that such things happen, nor is it only by Germans that they are done. If we wish to speak honestly of man as we have come to know him in our time, we dare not forget what we have learned of these demonic depths of human nature.

But what of *God*? That is the question with which we are confronted here today. Very bluntly put, the question is this: How can we believe any longer in a God of love and a God of power, a God who is "king of the universe," when six million Jews—almost the whole of European Jewry—could be slaughtered without the slightest sign of intervention, either from abroad or from above. (I am sure that the suffering inmates of the concentration camps would not have minded whether God worked mediately or immediately to save them—whether by lightening bolts from heaven or by the intervention of the U.S. government or of the papacy. *Neither* occurred.)

Here is the problem of theodicy on a cosmic scale. "Theodicy"—Leibnitz is thought to have coined the term, and the word itself contains the essence of our problem: how to reconcile our notion of God, *theos*, with our notion of justice, *dikē*. Or: how to justify the ways of God to man.

Put that way, the question sounds blasphemous; who is man that God should justify himself to him? Yet this is a question that is integral to biblical religion itself, from Job to St. Paul. Indeed, the problem of Auschwitz may be said to be *the problem of Job magnified six million-fold.*

It is significant that the profoundest treatment of the problem of evil in the Hebrew Bible is one that is couched in terms of a dramatic narrative about one single individual and his family. It is true also today that the terror and mystery of Auschwitz are brought home to us more by the story of one boy and one family, as told to us autobiographically by Elie Weisel, than by all the statistics or more generalized conclusions of those who have tried to analyze the problem as a whole. Perhaps this is because the human mind simply finds it impossible to work with both the *intensity* and *extensity* of the problem. Once one has entered to any extent into the suffering of one single individual caught in the nameless terror of the pogroms and the persecutions, the deportations and the death camps, it is difficult to multiply this, say, by sixtyfold and still retain one's grasp upon the problem. To multiply it by six hundredfold, by six thousandfold, by sixty thousandfold, by six hundred thousandfold, by six millionfold, is impossible. And so one's mind, reeling, returns to the picture of the single individual. We see him then, not only in himself, but as prototypical of the whole number of sufferers.

The figure of Job is pertinent to our inquiry above all for the chief characteristic with which the narrative endows him: his innocence. "There was a man in the land of Uz, whose name was Job; and that man was blameless and upright, one who feared God, and turned away from evil" (Job 1:1). It is this which gave the lie to the retributory doctrine represented by Job's friends—the idea that suffering is to be explained as the punishment for sin. Job protests his innocence, and in this he is vindicated, at the conclusion of the drama, by God himself. He does not claim to be wholly sinless; he is, after all, human. But he is in no way chargeable with transgressions of such a magnitude as to account for the suffering that is his. In this he is comparable to the victims of the Holocaust. For it is above all their innocence that is so moving, and so puzzling for a theodicy.

The doctrine of retribution dies hard, however. Note that it can work in two ways: (a) as a warning: "If you sin, you will suffer." This no doubt has some truth and can serve a useful hortatory purpose. But (b) it can also be used as an *ex post facto* explanation: "Because you are suffering, you must have sinned." Logically, this doesn't make sense. If all A is B, this in no way implies that all B is A. Psychologically, however, the retributory theory makes a great deal of "sense" in that it serves the sadistic impulse to increase the sufferings of others by adding to the suffering a further load of guilt for having brought it on oneself. Alternatively, it can serve masochistically to increase one's own suffering in this way.

How is God spoken of according to this theory? As a *God of judgment*, or even more, as a *God of vengeance*. The line between judgment and vengeance is this: in both, the suffering is related to antecedent sin; but "judgment" implies some reasonable proportion between the sin and the punishment, while "vengeance" implies a disproportion.

Is it possible to think of the Holocaust as God's judgment upon the Jews, or as his vengeance upon them? One's heart and mind and soul instinctively reject such a thought. Even to mention it is bitter to the tongue. Yet Christians must recognize that for centuries the church promoted just such a theory to explain the fall of Jerusalem and the destruction of the Jewish state. The besieging Romans, it was taught, were

God's instrument of judgment upon the Jews for not accepting the Messiah.

It is true that some Jewish thinkers themselves accepted the theory that Israel's suffering and its dispersal by the Romans was to be interpreted as punishment for its sins. That does not make the theory any more correct. Its inadequacies must be clearly exposed. Toward this end, the statement of the Second Vatican Council which lifts from the Jews and Judaism as such the charge of responsibility for the crucifixion makes a great contribution, as do the similar Lutheran statements. But much remains to be done through education among the broad masses of church membership to break the last threads of this guilt-and-punishment theory. This must be done as preventive therapy, lest at any time in the future there is a temptation to apply it once again.

If the doctrine of retribution was the chief theory represented by Job's interlocutors, there was also another theory, a subordinate motif, which we may call the *theory of moral education.* In a word, suffering is good for you! "Behold, happy is the man whom God reproves; therefore despise not the chastening of the Almighty. . . . He delivers the afflicted by their affliction, and opens their ear by adversity" (Job 5:17; 36:15). Again, this theory has some truth to it, but only a limited truth. It is a true statement of what a man of faith can make out of his suffering—but only up to a certain point. When his very humanity begins to be destroyed, as was the case in the concentration camps, then it is fruitless to talk of the ennoblement of his character.

In both these instances (the theory of retribution and the theory of moral education) we have a case of the extension of what Robert K. Merton, in another context, called "theories of the middle range" into all-inclusive explanatory principles; and that extension simply is not justified. If it were, it would leave us with the picture of a monstrous God who tortures his creatures in order to perfect them, a cosmic version of the American commander in Vietnam who declared that he had to "destroy the village in order to save it."

It is most interesting to discover that parallels to these two theories represented by Job's interlocutors echo down through the history of Christian thought. The most substantial recent volume dealing with this problem is John Hick's *Evil and the God of Love.*[2] Consulting Hick's

2. John Hick, *Evil and the God of Love* (New York: Harper and Row, 1966).

analysis, we find that he distinguishes between two major theories of evil (which is to say, two major types of theodicy) in Christian thought. The first he denominates the Augustinian theory, and the second the Irenaean, after the second century church father Irenaeus.

The Augustinian view is oriented to the categories of sin and punishment. The existence of suffering and evil in the world is attributable to the fall, i.e., to the fault of men. The Irenaean view, in contrast, looks not to the past but to the future for its explanation. It "finds the justification for evil in an infinite (because eternal) good which God is bringing out of the temporal process."[3] Life is a vale of soul-making, and all will eventually be to the good. Hick offers the following contrast between the two points of view:

> Instead of the [Augustinian] doctrine that man was created finitely perfect and then incomprehensibly destroyed his own perfection and plunged into sin and misery, Irenaeus suggests that man was created as an imperfect, immature creature who was to undergo moral development and growth and finally be brought to the perfection intended for him by his Maker. . . . Instead of the Augustinian view of life's trials as a divine punishment for Adam's sin, Irenaeus sees our world of mingled good and evil, as a divinely appointed environment for man's development. . . .[4]

Irenaeus's own words convey this "optimistic view" quite graphically:

> How, if we had no knowledge of the contrary, could we have had instruction in that which is good? . . . For just as the tongue receives experience of sweet and bitter by means of tasting, and the eye discriminates between black and white by means of vision . . . so also does the mind, receiving through the experience of both the knowledge of what is good, become more tenacious of its preservation, by acting in obedience to God.[5]

A very interesting theory, but in no way sufficient as an explanation of the Holocaust.

Those who are acquainted with the thought of Teilhard de Chardin will recognize that he stands within this Irenaean tradition. All of life tends toward the Omega Point, and is justified in its partial value by that total fulfillment toward which all things move. An inspiring cosmic

3. Hick, *Evil and the God of Love*, p. 263.
4. *Ibid.*, pp. 220 ff.
5. Irenaeus *Against Heresies* 4.1. Quoted by Hick, *Evil and the God of Love* p. 220.

vision—but one that is only able to deal with the tragedies along the way by, in effect, minimizing them. Teilhard has been widely criticized for being unable to interpret in terms of his cosmic evolutionary theory the tragic events of the twentieth century, which seem to have thrown into reverse what might have appeared to the nineteenth century as human progress.

If the first theory speaks of God as *the God of judgment*, the second speaks of God as *the God of creative purpose*. But neither is adequate to explain, much less to justify, Auschwitz. Neither, in fact, was found adequate by Job to explain his own suffering. The only answer Job receives is the theophany: an experience of the overwhelming majesty and awfulness of God. In this sense, the answer to Job's question is that there is no answer: I am God and you are man; and the fact that you are man is reflected precisely in the fact that you cannot comprehend my ways. Job bows to the dust, in humility and faith.

What does this mean for our speaking about God? It means that we speak of God as *the God of mystery*; that we acknowledge the inscrutability of God.

If we return to John Hick's analysis for a moment, we find that although he adopts, on the whole, the Irenaean viewpoint that the sufferings of this present time are justified by their eventual result, it is precisely the Holocaust which he acknowledges cannot be fit within this context of explanation. He has to allow it to remain as a surd, as something unexplainable.

It is to be noted as a grievous failing of Hick's whole study that in a four hundred page volume on "Evil and the God of Love," published in 1966, he does not refer to the Holocaust until page 397! His discussion up to this point is altogether too much in the domain of the personal, the psychological, and the metaphysical rather than the historical and the political realms. If he had taken this greatest example of the upsurge of evil in modern times into account earlier in his analysis, it might have affected the whole result; it might have destroyed the relative optimism of his Irenaean viewpoint.

Nevertheless, when he does refer to the Holocaust, he does not balk at describing it for what it is. Hick has been describing the way in which we are helped to bear our own suffering when we understand it within the context of God's ultimate loving purpose. "What, however," he asks, "of the sins and sufferings of others?" And he continues:

> When we ask such a question today we almost inevitably think of the Nazi programme for the extermination of the Jewish people, with all the brutality and bestial cruelty that it involved and evoked. What does that ultimate purpose of divine purpose and activity mean for Auschwitz and Belsen and the other camps in which, between 1942 and 1945, between four and six million Jewish men, women, and children were deliberately and scientifically murdered? Was this in any sense willed by God?
>
> The answer is obviously no. These events were utterly evil, wicked, devilish and, so far as the human mind can reach, unforgiveable; they are wrongs that can never be righted, horrors which will disfigure the universe to the end of time, and in relation to which no condemnation can be strong enough, no revulsion adequate. . . . Most certainly God did not want those who committed these fearful crimes against humanity to act as they did. His purpose for the world was retarded by them and the power of evil within it increased.[6]

Thus Hick can offer no explanation for the Holocaust. The most he can offer is a word of hope and consolation regarding the individuals who were caught up in it. His words to this effect are worth a further extended quotation.

> Our Christian awareness of the universal divine purpose and activity does, however, affect our reaction even to these events. First, as regards the millions of men, women, and children who perished in the extermination programme, it gives the assurance that God's purpose for each individual has not been defeated by the efforts of wicked men. In the realms beyond our world they are alive and will have their place in the final fulfillment of God's creation. The transforming importance of the Christian hope of eternal life—not only for oneself but for all men—has already been stressed above, and is vitally relevant here.
>
> Secondly within the situation itself, the example of Christ's self-giving love for others should have led Christians to be willing to risk their own lives to help the escape of the threatened victims; and here the record is partly good but also, unhappily, in too large part bad. And third, a Christian faith should neutralize the impulse to meet hatred and cruelty with an answering hatred and cruelty. . . . Such a renouncing of the satisfaction of vengeance may be made possible to our sinful hearts by the knowledge that the inevitable reaction of a moral universe upon cruelty will be met, within this life or beyond it, without our aid. "Vengeance is mine, I will repay, says the Lord."[7]

Thus Hick has recourse to a doctrine of eschatological reward and retribution, and he ends, as we began, with a reference to the God of ven-

6. Hick, *Evil and the God of Love*, p. 397.
7. *Ibid.*, pp. 397 f.

geance; now, however, not of vengeance upon the Jews, but upon their oppressors.

Without entering into a discussion of that motif as such, let us observe once more that in this major effort at a theodicy by a contemporary Christian theologian, he cannot comprehend the Holocaust within his framework of explanation. We are thus left to speak of God, so far as his relation to this event is concerned, in terms of mystery. Like Job, we bow in awe before his inscrutability.

There is a category in Lutheran theology which is intended as an acknowledgment of this mystery, this inscrutability. This is the notion of the *Deus absconditus*—the hidden God. Luther derived the phrase from the Latin of Isa. 45:15: *Vere, tu es Deus absconditus.* "Truly, thou art a God that hidest thyself."

For Luther, the will of God is not evident in the ordinary course of world events. His will is known only where he chooses to make it known; only in revelatory moments, not in life as a whole. We live by those moments, but in so doing, we walk by faith, not by sight. And faith is usually contrary to experience.

We spoke of the *Deus absconditus* as a category in Lutheran thought. It is more than a category: it is the background or undertone of all that is said in this theology. It was Miguel de Unamuno, I believe, who coined the phrase "the tragic sense of life"; but we may say that Luther, above all other theologians, possessed this tragic sense. All his assertions of faith, of courage, and of victory were rooted in what one Luther interpreter has called "the grand nevertheless." *Trotzdem*—in spite of all—I will believe!

Let us recapitulate the discussion thus far. The problem of Auschwitz, like the problem of evil as such, is the problem of how such things can happen if God is both good and powerful. If he is not good, then he looks upon these matters with indifference or even, if this is conceivable, with delight. But such a God would in no way be the God we worship. Luther suggests that the very word *Gott* ("God") is rooted in the concept of *Gut* ("good"). *Gut und Gott*: the two cannot be torn apart, or all that we know as Christian or Jewish faith would turn into its opposite. If the goodness of God is not to be given up, if he is truly all-loving and at the same time all-powerful, then Auschwitz cannot be explained. It remains in the domain of mystery. It is not surprising, therefore, that attention has been paid to the other pole of the equation, and it has been asked, Is God in fact all-powerful, or in what sense is he all-powerful?

We enter here upon a realm of theological questions which we can in no way treat adequately within the framework of the present paper. We can only briefly pass in review some of the major forms which reflection about this question has taken—the question being that of the nature and limits of God's power or of the exercise thereof.

The first is the conception of a finite God. This is a notion which, needless to say, has never found residence in any body of official Christian teaching. The idea no doubt has a long history. In American theology, its chief spokesman, in fact its sole spokesman of any prominence, was Professor Edgar Sheffield Brightman of Boston University. Brightman posited an element which he called "the Given," with which God himself has to deal, either using it as an instrument or, if that is impossible, acknowledging it as an obstacle.

> The Given consists of the eternal uncreated laws of reason and also of equally eternal and uncreated processes of nonrational consciousness, . . . disorderly impulses and desires, such experiences as pain and suffering, the forms of space and time, and whatever in God is the source of surd evil.[8]

The last sentence is significant. By "surd evil" Brightman means evil that is *not* explainable as the means to a greater good. He speaks of this as having its source "in God"; yet it constitutes for God a limit upon his own nature, a limit upon his will to love.

Brightman's view, as we have already indicated, has found little if any acceptance. I mention it precisely because it is so little known, and yet so precisely directed to our problem.

The second view of which we must take note speaks not of a finite God, but of a self-limited God. Unlike Brightman's conception, this one has a long and venerable history in Christian thought, and indeed in Jewish thought as well. I am speaking of God's self-limitation simply in this sense: in that he has created a world with two interrelated characteristics—freedom and lawfulness. Man is free: free to choose good or evil. But nature is bound, bound to act in accordance with cause and effect. Thus man is free to conceive and to construct the gas chambers at Auschwitz. And when the handle is turned, gas will flow through the

8. Edgar Sheffield Brightman, *A Philosophy of Religion* (New York: Prentice-Hall, 1940), p. 337.

nozzle. God is powerless, unless he wishes to contravene either human freedom or physical natural law. And this he does not wish to do.

Involved here is the whole question of grace and free will, of providence and predestination, indeed a whole metaphysic and a whole theology. My purpose here is simply to suggest that the problem of "speaking of God after Auschwitz" can hardly be dealt with apart from this range of considerations. It is a question that goes to the heart of our conception of God and man, and of their relations one to the other.

Speaking quite personally, I should have to say this: that in an intellectual sense, this solution (that of a self-limiting God) may be satisfying; but in a religious sense, and in a moral sense, it is not. For when the horrors grow so extreme as was the case in Auschwitz, then one's conscience cries out for God, if necessary, to put an end to history itself to stop the slaughter.

Yet, on further reflection, we may not really wish that. When we consider the relative meaningfulness of our own lives despite the pall of sadness from such horrors as the Holocaust, and when we consider the resurrection of Israel itself after the catastrophe—that is, the return of the Jews to their ancient homeland and their rebirth as a nation—we realize that we would *not* have wanted history to stop at some point in the early 1940s. And so we sympathize, if one may say so, with the dilemma in which God found himself, and in which he continually finds himself, confronted with a world which he has chosen to endow with mixed characteristics of freedom and lawfulness.

We have spoken of the finite God and the self-limited God. The third conception is that of the embattled God. I am speaking here of views that posit a demonic force that struggles against the divine. Paul Tillich may be credited with reintroducing the concept of the demonic into contemporary theology. It represents a demythologized version of the traditional notion of the devil, or Satan. There is no personal devil, but the demonic is terribly real. It consists in what Tillich has called "structures of destruction"—forces, trends, powers, irrational movements and instances of mass hysteria, all leading to the awful possibility of the pursuit of evil simply for evil's sake.

The rediscovery of this factor was not in the first instance an intellectual event; it was a historical event, based on the outcropping in the twentieth century of the dark underground of human history. Paul Tillich had the prescience to articulate this concept already in the 1920s, on the basis both of his experience in the First World War, and also on the basis of his long-term analysis of trends in modern life and thought that were to coalesce in the phenomenon of Nazism, and that had already begun to gain momentum in that very decade. His estimate of Nazism and his struggle against it were very clear, so much so that when the Nazis assumed power in 1933, the name of Paul Tillich was on the very first list of university professors to be dismissed from their posts.

The rediscovery of the demonic has had a tremendous impact on our image of man, since it is through man that the demonic works. But it also has an impact on our concept of God. It causes us to think of God as an embattled God, still struggling against the powers of evil in the world. Among Lutheran theologians, Gustaf Aulén has been prominent among those giving voice to this conception. He was professor of theology at the University of Lund and later a bishop of the Church of Sweden.

Aulén, in his book *Christus Victor*[9] and in his systematic theology, has set forth a dualistic-dramatic theory of the atonement. It is dualistic in that it posits a radical opposition between God and the powers of evil. It is dramatic in that it sees this opposition as working itself out on the stage of history in terms of the concrete clash between destructive and constructive powers. It is a theory of the atonement in that it posits a decisive significance for the event of Christ, seeing in his crucifixion and resurrection the decisive battle in this warfare between the divine and the demonic.

Aulén and others in the period after the Second World War used to employ the following illustration. Our present situation in history, they said, after the resurrection and before the parousia—that is, between the "first" and "second" comings—is like the situation of occupied Europe when the successful Allied invasion of Normandy was announced. The people of occupied Europe knew at that point that their liberation was at hand. Indeed, the victory had already begun, and even though setbacks might yet occur, the final triumph of the Allied cause was certain. So it is, said these Christian theologians, in the interim between the advent of the Messiah and the total victory of his kingdom. We live between D-Day and V-Day.

This theory, it may be pointed out, can be read in either of two ways. It is like the proverbial half-full glass of water, which may equally well be viewed as half-empty. On the one hand, there is a note of confidence

9. Gustaf Aulén, *Christus Victor* (New York: Macmillan, 1956).

in what God has done. On the other hand, there is a very sober realism about the battles that may yet lie ahead. To speak in this way of God is to speak of an embattled God. But that is perhaps to accentuate the negative. Let us speak more positively and biblically, with a slight turn of the phrase, by speaking rather of a "God of battles."

We have reviewed three "solutions" to our problem which left the divine sovereignty unimpaired, but thereby failed to answer the question of how the reality of God and the fact of Auschwitz can be held together. These were the sin-and-punishment theory, the character-education theory, and the theory that declines to answer the question, leaving the matter in the realm of mystery. Then we surveyed three positions which in some way do qualify God's sovereignty, at least with respect to the present age. These were the theories of the finite God, the self-limited God, and the embattled God.

With all this, however, we still have not spoken of God in the way that corresponds most closely to the nature of the problem, and that corresponds too to the deepest insights of the Christian—and also, I believe, of the Jewish—faith. This is to speak of the suffering God.

The late Abraham Joshua Heschel taught us to speak of the "divine pathos." He reminded us of how different is the Greek concept of God dwelling alone in *apatheia* ("without feeling"), or "thinking on thinking," from the Hebraic conception of a living and active God who is vitally concerned with the affairs of men. Heschel urged us not to be afraid to speak of God—not anthropomorphically to be sure—but "anthropopathically." God too knows wrath and love and jealousy and joy, according to the Bible. If the danger of this line of thinking is God's humanization, even worse, said Heschel, would be his anaesthetization.

Above all it is Jeremiah, according to Heschel's study of the prophets, who taught us of God's involvement in the sufferings of men. It is intriguing to note that precisely the same point is made by the Japanese theologian Kazoh Kitamori in his book *Theology of the Pain of God*. This work, published in English translation in 1965,[10] is believed to be the first work of Christian theology ever translated from Japanese into English, rather than the other way around. Kitamori writes:

10. Kazoh Kitamori, *Theology of the Pain of God* (Richmond: John Knox Press, 1965).

> It is said that Isaiah saw God's holiness, Hosea saw God's love, and Amos saw God's righteousness. We wish to add that Jeremiah saw God's pain. . . .[11]

This is a pain, says Kitamori, which is at the same time God's love.

This is for me, religiously, the solution to the problem. God participates in the sufferings of men, and man is called to participate in the sufferings of God. Perhaps it is the only adequate solution intellectually as well. It was the German philosopher Friedrich Schelling who said in his book *Of Human Freedom*, that "all of history is virtually an enigma without a concept of an agonizing God." That, I think, is a memorable statement.[12]

For Christianity, the symbol of the agonizing God is the cross of Christ. I think that it is tragic that this symbol should have become a symbol of division between Jews and Christians, for the reality to which it points is a Jewish reality as well. I mean the reality of suffering and martyrdom.

The cross is not the instrument upon which the Jews put Jesus or anyone else to death; it was the Roman overlords who did so. Rather, the cross was the instrument upon which Jews were put to death. And this long antedates the time of Jesus. According to Josephus, Cyrus introduced into his edict for the return of the Jews from Babylon the threat of crucifixion for any who interfered with the execution of his edict. Darius the Persian threatened this death to those who refused obedience to his decrees. Antiochus Epiphanes crucified faithful Jews who would not abandon their religion at his bidding. And after the siege of Jerusalem by the Romans, Titus crucified so many Jews that, says Josephus, "there was not enough room for the crosses, nor enough crosses for the condemned."[13]

The cross thus refers in the first instance to a *Jewish* reality: to the reality of suffering, all too well known to this people, from the time when they cried out in their affliction under Pharaoh, down to the time of their

11. *Ibid.*, p. 161.

12. This wording is taken from the English version of Kitamori's book, and is presumably a translation of the Japanese translation of Schelling. The reference is to *Of Human Freedom*, p. 403 of the German original; in the English translation by James Gutmann (Chicago: Open Court, 1936), it reads: "All history remains incomprehensible without the concept of a humanly suffering God."

13. Josephus *The Jewish War* 5.11.2.451. Quoted by Maurice Goguel, *The Life of Jesus,* tr. Olive Wyon (London: Allen & Unwin, 1933), p. 534.

yet more unspeakable sufferings under the modern Pharaoh. The further interpretations which Christians give to the cross of Christ are well known, but what I wish to do is to point us back behind the interpretations to the reality of this man who suffered as a Jew, and on the basis of whose sufferings the Christian should be the first to identify with the sufferings of any Jews.

The fact that this has not been the case, and that the cross has been the symbol not of identification but of inquisition, is a matter for the deepest shame on the part of Christianity. One thing is clear as to how we may speak of God after Auschwitz. We may not speak, and we cannot speak, in terms of any kind of triumphalism. We can speak only in repentance. A God who suffers is the opposite of a God of triumphalism. We can speak of God after Auschwitz only as the one who calls us to a new unity as beloved brothers—not only between Jews and Christians, but especially between them.

At an interfaith service held at the Lutheran School of Theology at Chicago on May 29, 1973, to commemorate the thirtieth anniversary of the Warsaw uprising, a prayer was offered which expresses very well this spirit of repentance and renewal. It was said antiphonally between the leader and the congregation:

> With those who grade any people as "superior" or "inferior" . . .
> *We share the guilt, O Lord.*
> With those who would "solve" any problem by destroying a group . . .
> *We share the guilt, O Lord.*
> With those who pretend not to know what a leader who traffics in fear and hatred will do . . .
> *We share the guilt, O Lord.*
> With those who exult when their group does what they individually would be ashamed to do . . .
> *We share the guilt, O Lord.*
> With those who wait until defeat to condemn what they accept in victory . . .
> *We share the guilt, O Lord.*
> We share the guilt, and ask your help, O Lord . . .
> *To stand today against what we condemned a generation ago.*
> We share the guilt, and ask your help, O Lord . . .
> *To stand in our own country against what we condemn in another.*
> We share the guilt, and ask your help, O Lord . . .

To know that what all evil persons have done, we too could do.
We share the guilt, and ask your help, O Lord . . .
To know that what all good and brave persons have done, we too could do.
We share the guilt . . .
And the glory, O Lord.
In the holocaust . . .
May the I-who-am-opposed-to-you be consumed.
From the ashes of the holocaust . . .
May the I-who-am-with-you arise.[14]

We have surveyed various aspects of the question of "Speaking of God after the Holocaust." Perhaps much of this speculation has been futile. In conclusion, we may refer to Karl Marx's famous remark in the last of his "Theses on Feuerbach." "The philosophers," he said, "have only *interpreted* the world, in various ways; the point, however, is to *change* it."

It may be questioned whether it is proper at all to employ God as an explanatory hypothesis, as some of the thinkers whom we have surveyed have done. God is not in the first instance an explanatory hypothesis; he is an impelling force. The very best way to speak of God after Auschwitz, therefore, is to speak of him in such a way that men are moved to see to it that such a thing never happens again. Unfortunately, in a world in which human freedom and human perversity are both very real, we cannot say that it *could* not happen. Therefore we say that it *must* not happen.

We have treated the problem of the Holocaust, as our topic demanded, in terms of the problem of God. But we need to return from this ultimate level of the question to the proximate level, on which the phenomenon of the Holocaust will be treated in terms of its more immediate historical causes. That is a task, however, not for one or two brief sessions of a conference, but for an ongoing inquiry that, despite all the work that has already been done, will require yet more years and decades until the significance of this event is really understood. Let us as Jews and Christians dedicate ourselves to joint participation in that ongoing task.

14. The author of this litany is Robert Blakely.

APPENDICES

Some Observations and Guidelines for Conversations between Lutherans and Jews[1]

Improved relationships among separated Christian churches in recent decades have also led to growing conversation between Jewish and Christian groups. We commend all endeavors which seek greater understanding, mutual confidence, elimination of tensions, and cooperation in the quest for justice and peace, and note statements issued by Lutheran groups which are helpful in these areas.[2]

Amid the pluralism of American society today and in the face of many practical problems facing Christians, Jews, and all men of good will, it is especially necessary to foster and expand such conversations on more local levels, as a contribution to community understanding and cooperation, to heal wounds of the past, and to understand better our common heritage and common humanity. Today the mission of the church surely includes such conversations, and indeed must often begin with them. We urge Lutheran pastors, people, and institutions to seek greater involvement in such endeavors.

The Christian cannot fully understand what it means to be Jewish but our common ground in humanity and in the Hebrew Scriptures makes a base for beginning. In order to have authentic relationships there must be honesty, openness, frankness, and mutual respect along with a recognition of the real differences that exist and a willingness to risk confronting these differences.

To these ends we offer some practical suggestions and make some observations as to methods so that conversation may be both honest and fruitful.

1. This document was prepared by the Division of Theological Studies, Lutheran Council in the U.S.A., at the request of the Council's Executive Committee. It was transmitted in April, 1971, to the church bodies participating in the Lutheran Council: the American Lutheran Church, the Lutheran Church in America, and the Lutheran Church—Missouri Synod.

2. E.g., "The Church and the Jewish People" (see pp. 166–173 below).

1. In localities where Lutherans are comparatively few in number, they are encouraged to cooperate with other Christian groups in initiating and sustaining conversation with Jews.
2. Where Lutherans comprise a substantial group within a locality, they are encouraged to take the initiative in fostering conversation and community understanding.
3. Meetings should be jointly planned so as to avoid any suspicion of proselyting and to lessen the danger of offense through lack of sensitivity or accurate information about the other group.
4. Because of the long history of alienation between the two groups, Christians and Jews should remember that one meeting does little more than set the stage for serious conversations. False hopes and superficial optimism by either group can lead to despair and further alienation.
5. On both sides, living communities of faith and worship are involved. Because of fervent commitments emotions may run deep. It should be underscored that neither polemics nor conversions are the aim of such conversations, nor is false irenicism or mere surface agreement. There may remain honest differences, even as broad areas of agreement are discovered.
6. If we have been open and have shared our assumptions, prejudices, traditions, and convictions, we may be able to share in realistic goal setting, especially in regard to further understanding and common cause in spiritual and social concerns such as fostering human rights.
7. Different methods of procedure may be followed as mutually determined locally, such as:
   a. Educational visits to advance mutual understanding of artistic, liturgical tradition.
   b. Exchange of visits at regular worship services, "open houses," and special celebrations, followed by explanation and discussion.
   c. Informal small group discussions in homes in the manner of the "living room dialogues." Participants may involve one synagogue and one congregation or neighborhood groups without regard to membership.
   d. Weekend retreats with equal participation of members from both groups and equality of expertise.
   e. Popular lectures, discussion, and demonstrations by well-informed resource persons. Lutherans might invite representa-

tives of the American Jewish Committee, Jewish Chatauqua Society, Anti-Defamation League of B'nai B'rith, National Conference of Christians and Jews, and Jewish theological schools.

f. Scholarly lectures and discussions by experts in biblical, historical, and theological studies.

8. Possible topics include: Our Common Heritage; The People of God and Covenant; Christian and Jewish Views of Man; The Significance of Hebrew Scriptures Today; Law, Righteousness, and Justice; State of Israel; The Christian Church in Israel; Survey of the Attitudes and Teachings of the Church Concerning Judaism; The Image of the Jew in Christian Literature; Luther and the Jews; The Meaning of Suffering; Can a Hebrew Christian be a Jew? An Israeli?; Eschatology in Christian and Jewish Theology; The Significance of the Septuagint; The Universal God in an Age of Pluralism; The State and the Religious Community in Jewish and Lutheran Traditions; What Can We Do Together?
9. Christians should make it clear that there is no biblical or theological basis for anti-Semitism. Supposed theological or biblical bases for anti-Semitism are to be examined and repudiated. Conscious or unconscious manifestations of discrimination are to be opposed.

The Church and the Jewish People[1]

I. The Church and Israel

The church may use the term Israel theologically only in the sense in which it appears in the Scriptures of the Old and New Testaments: in the first instance, as an expression of God's sovereign grace toward Abraham and his descendants, the people of the old covenant, to whom God revealed his will and promised his redemption for the blessing of the nations; in the second place, as an expression for the people of the new covenant made up of Jews and gentiles in which, through the redemption in Jesus Christ, the gentiles become fellow heirs of the promises. Here we take up both the New Testament assertions about the true seed of Abraham and the typological interpretations of Old Testament history as applied to the church.

Thus the church testifies that, by the fulfillment of the promises in Jesus the Messiah and by his acceptance by but a part of the Jews, a division has arisen which has placed the "old" Israel outside the "new." This division will be healed when "all Israel" (Rom. 11:26) recognizes Jesus of Nazareth as its Messiah. Only then will the mystery of the faithfulness of God toward his people be resolved. Those who share in the inheritance must recognize a grateful responsibility for the original heirs. It follows, therefore, that the church will pray for the Jews daily, especially in its Sunday worship.

Those who in faith through baptism have put on Christ Jesus are all Christians, without distinction, whether they have their origin in the people of the old covenant or among the gentiles. Terms such as "Hebrew Christian," and the like, introduce unbiblical divisions into the church.

1. Parts I-III of this document were prepared at a Consultation on the Church and the Jews, convened by the Lutheran World Federation's Department of World Mission at Løgumkloster, Denmark, in 1964. Part IV represents subsequent study by a Committee on the Church and the Jews, which completed its work at a meeting in Geneva, Switzerland, in 1969. The document was presented to the meeting of the LWF Commission on World Mission in Asmara, Ethiopia, that same year, and to the Fifth Assembly of the LWF in Evian, France, in July, 1970.

The gathering of Jews in the land of the patriarchs may in God's redemptive purposes have special importance. We live much too close to this development, however, to make a specific judgment about its religious significance: God's action in history we are unable to discern.

II. Mission and Dialogue

A. The church is called by its Lord to be his body in the world, and to proclaim the mighty works of God to all men (Acts 2:11). Following the call of its Lord, the church has the responsibility of beseeching all men on behalf of Christ to be reconciled to God (2 Cor. 5:20). Because of this responsibility, the church also has the obligation to carry on organized mission activities through which the message of reconciliation is brought to men. As a member of the body of Christ, every Christian also shares in the "sent-ness" of the church. This quality of "being sent" applies in every area of the Christian's relationship to the world, and he will witness with his whole life in testifying to his faith (1 Pet. 3:15), in listening to others, in seeking to understand, and in sharing the burdens of his fellowman.

B. The witness to the Jewish people is inherent in the content of the gospel, and in the commission received from Christ, the head of the church. The mission will most effectively reflect the glory of Christ in his gospel when it is pursued in the normal activity of the Christian congregation, which reflects itself in the Christian witness of the individual members. Where Jewish communities in the world cannot normally be reached by Christian congregations, mission organizations must provide for the proclamation of the gospel to these people.

C. It is a Christian responsibility to seek respectfully to understand both the Jewish people and their faith. Therefore responsible conversations between Christians and Jews are to be desired and welcomed. Such conversations presuppose the existence of common ground on which Christians and Jews may meet, as well as points of difference. The conversations may be carried on through organized institutes, or by individuals and groups. The conversations do not assume an equating of the religions, nor do they require that Christians abstain from making their witness as a natural outgrowth of the discussions. Similarly Christians will listen gladly as Jews explain their insights of faith.

III. The Church and Anti-Semitism

Anti-Semitism is an estrangement of man from his fellowmen. As such it stems from human prejudice and is a denial of the dignity and equality of men. But anti-Semitism is primarily a denial of the image of God in the Jews; it represents a demonic form of rebellion against the God of Abraham, Isaac, and Jacob, and a rejection of Jesus the Jew, directed upon his people. "Christian" anti-Semitism is spiritual suicide. This phenomenon presents a unique question to the Christian church, especially in light of the long and terrible history of Christian culpability for anti-Semitism. No Christian can exempt himself from involvement in this guilt. As Lutherans, we confess our own peculiar guilt, and we lament with shame the responsibility which our church and her people bear for this sin. We can only ask God's pardon and that of the Jewish people.

There is no ultimate defeat of anti-Semitism short of a return to the living God in the power of his grace and through the forgiveness of Jesus Christ our Lord. At the same time, we must pledge ourselves to work in concert with others at practical measures for overcoming manifestations of this evil within and without the church and for reconciling Christians with Jews.

Toward this end, we urge the Lutheran World Federation and its member churches:

1. To examine their publications for possible anti-Semitic references, and to remove and oppose false generalizations about Jews. Especially reprehensible are the notions that Jews, rather than all mankind, are responsible for the death of Jesus the Christ, and that God has for this reason rejected his covenant people. Such examination and reformation must also be directed to pastoral practice and preaching references. This is our simple duty under the commandment common to Jews and Christians: "Thou shalt not bear false witness against thy neighbor."

2. To oppose and work to prevent all national and international manifestations of anti-Semitism, and in all our work acknowledge our great debt of gratitude to those Jewish people who have been instruments of the Holy Spirit in giving us the Old and New Testaments and in bringing into the world Jesus Christ our Lord.

3. To call upon our congregations and people to know and to love their Jewish neighbors as themselves; to fight against discrimination or persecution of Jews in their communities; to develop mutual understand-

ing; and to make common cause with the Jewish people in matters of spiritual and social concern, especially in fostering human rights.

IV. On the Theology of the Church's Relation to Judaism

1. We as Christians can only speak of the Jewish people if we say that we are all human beings standing under God's judgment and in need of his forgiveness. We are all men and women before we are Jews and Christians. What we say here in a special way about the Jews must be understood in the light of this assertion.

The relationship between Jews and Christians has been confused through the centuries by two wrong assumptions. The first assumption falsifies the Christian understanding by seeing the Jews of all times as identical with that Jewish group which in the first century rejected Jesus of Nazareth as Messiah. The second falsifies the Jewish understanding by seeing all Christians as in principle involved in the hate and persecution which were inflicted on the Jews by the official church and by nations claiming a Christian tradition. While this Committee claims no competence to remove the existing negative opinions held by Jews, it must contribute to the task of eliminating all those barriers raised by past and present Christian misunderstanding which stand in the way of our conversation with the Jews and our understanding of their faith.

We shall have to engage in an ongoing encounter with Jews and Judaism which takes seriously both Jewish and Christian history. In deepening the Jewish-Christian relationship we expect to find ways of understanding each other which have been lost due to historical circumstances. Theological education—and the teaching of church history in particular—will have to undergo considerable revision if this is to be done. Teachers and pastors must be given information and materials so that in their interpreting of biblical texts they will be sensitive to the false assumptions Christians have made.

The distinction between law and gospel which in Lutheran tradition becomes a key for interpreting the whole scriptural revelation is connected with this hermeneutical problem. This specific emphasis places a particular burden on Jewish-Lutheran relations. But for this reason it lends increased urgency to theological encounter. As Lutherans we believe, on the basis of Paul's witness, that it is God's action in Christ which justifies the sinner. Thus we cannot speak about the law and about righteousness as though it were obedience which lays the foundation for relationship to God. The theological issue here touches both Jewish-Christian dialogue and Christian use of the Old Testament. Our understanding can be traced to Luther and his reception through Augustine of certain Pauline motifs. It is possible, however, that our whole outlook has been shaped and our relationship to the Jewish people has been vitiated by a strongly negative understanding of the law and its function. This, it seems to us, might well be a matter for consideration by the Lutheran World Federation Commission on Theology in cooperation with a possible future Committee on the Church and the Jews.

2. As we try to grasp the theological meaning of the problem we face, we recognize two aspects of the Christian understanding of God's self-disclosure, both of which lead us to the limits of human perception and speech. The first is the fact that with the coming of Jesus into the world a development began which is incomprehensible in its dimensons. It can only be described as an act of God's love for all men. In the moment when, according to Christian faith, God acted to bring his revelation to its fulfillment, among those who had first received his revelation many did not find themselves able to respond in faith to what God was now doing in Jesus of Nazareth. In spite of this rejection, however, God's saving grace found a way into the world and no human guilt or rejection could negate it. The faith and the universal proclamation that God became man, that God was in Christ reconciling the world unto himself, that Jesus of Nazareth was the Son of God, is an offense to human wisdom and particularly to the religious view of God's glory. It is as if God had of necessity to meet rejection and to suffer the consequences of his love in order to bring life and salvation to mankind.

The second aspect is closely related to the first. Because Jesus took upon himself his cross and became obedient unto death, God raised him from the dead. His death and resurrection constitute a special Christian hope for the whole world. This implies the crucial paradox that for the Christian faith there is a divine future for mankind since Jesus the Nazarene was rejected. Thus we are here directed toward the mystery of God's inscrutable ways with men.

Mystery and paradox—the point where human logic leads no further—stand at the center of all Christian thought. That is the case with Christology, but it is equally true of eschatology, and it applies to ecclesiology as well. God has not only prepared a future for all mankind, but has bound this future to the cross and resurrection of the man Jesus of Nazareth. It is our conviction that the central position of the cross and resurrection of Jesus has fundamental consequences for the understanding of the church. This was perceived and expressed in a unique way by Luther. He did not accept identification of the elect people of God with a specific ecclesiological tradition. This view has led to the fatal alternatives of medieval church-centered theology, in which the Jewish people were treated from a position of superiority. Luther opposed any kind of a "theology of glory," i.e., any attempt to see and proclaim God and his deeds and works (including the church) primarily in terms of might, of lordship, of victory and triumph. The theological paradox which confronted Luther in his historical situation, however, proved to be too much for him. This one can see from his later writings against the Jews. In these polemic tracts a theology of glory does break in. Luther's anxiety about the church's existence became so strong that he found himself no longer able to let the future rest in God's hands but, in anticipation of what he read to be God's future judgment, called upon the secular arm to effect that judgment in the present. In doing so he overstepped the bounds of what it lies in human authority to do, to say nothing of love. The consequences of this are still with us. The lessons which the church has had to learn in the midst of the holocausts of our century compel us to find a new, more profound, more sober, and at the same time more Christian attitude.

Because of the deep and tragic involvement of men of Christian tradition in the persecution of the Jewish people, the cruel and dangerous anti-Jewish attacks in some of the writings of the old Luther, and the continuing threats in our time to the existence of the Jews as a community, we assert our Christian responsibility for their right to exist as Jews.

3. Jews, on their side, insist that there can be mutual respect and dialogue only if the "legitimacy" of Judaism is recognized by Christians. We believe that this includes not only ethnic and political but also religious factors. What does it mean for us to acknowledge its "legitimacy"? Remembering past Christian criticism of Judaism, Jews demand of Christians recognition of Judaism as a "living" religion. Can such recognition be given? Does it mean that we see two separate but necessary ministries within the one economy of salvation? Is it possible to acknowledge that the survival of Judaism is an act of God without also saying that this survival is a definitive event of salvation history? Does affirmation of the survival or acknowledgment of the legitimacy of Judaism cancel the responsibility of the Christian to bear witness to the Jew at the right time and in the proper way?

In the light of these questions we offer the following affirmations:

We as Lutherans affirm our solidarity with the Jewish people. This solidarity is legitimized in God's election and calling into being in Abraham's seed a people of promise, of faith, and of obedience peculiar unto him, a people whose unity will one day become manifest when "all Israel" will be saved. The Lutheran churches, therefore, may not so appropriate the term "people of God" and "Israel" to the church in such a way as to deny that they applied in the first instance to the Jewish people. They may not assert that continuity of the church with the covenant people of Abraham in such a way as to question the fact that present-day Judaism has its own continuity with Old Testament Israel.

Thus our solidarity with the Jewish people is to be affirmed not only despite the crucifixion of Jesus, but also because of it. Through his death Jesus has brought about reconciliation with God, has broken down the barriers between men, and has established a ministry of reconciliation which encompasses all men, both Jews and gentiles.

Thus our solidarity with the Jewish people is grounded in God's unmerited grace, his forgiveness of sin and his justification of the disobedient. Whenever we Christians, therefore, speak about "rejection" and "faith," "disobedience" and "obedience," in such a way that "rejection" and "disobedience" are made to be attributes of Jews while "faith" and "obedience" are made to be attributes of Christians, we are not only guilty of the most despicable spiritual pride, but we foster a pernicious slander, denying the very ground of our own existence: grace, forgiveness, and justification.

After all that has happened, the existence of the Jewish people in the world today cannot therefore be seen in the first instance as a problem to be encountered, much less as an embarrassment to be faced by the churches, but as a profound cause for wonder and hope. Despite all the inhuman actions of men and the frightful ambiguities of history, God remains faithful to his promise. We have here tangible evidence that God's grace is yet at work countering the demonic powers of destruction and guaranteeing a future for mankind which will bring the full unity of God's people.

In understanding ourselves as people of the new covenant which God has made in Jesus the Christ, we Christians see the Jewish people as a reminder of our origin, as a partner in dialogue to understand our common history, and as a living admonition that we too are a pilgrim people, a people enroute toward a goal that can only be grasped in hope. The church, therefore, may never so understand the Word which has been entrusted to it, the Baptism which it must administer, and the Holy Supper which it has been commanded to celebrate as possessions which give Christians superiority over the Jews. The church can only administer in humility the mysteries which God has committed to it—preaching the crucified and risen Christ, baptizing into his death, showing forth his death till he come.

The word which our churches, in bearing witness to Jesus the Christ, must share with Jews as with other men is a joyful message of imperishable hope. This message shows forth a time when God's purpose with his covenant in Abraham and with his covenant in Jesus the Christ will be fulfilled. Then God overcomes all blindness, faithlessness, and disobedience and will be all in all.

BIBLIOGRAPHY

Bibliography

The footnotes of the essays in this volume contain references to a number of books and articles useful in pursuing Jewish-Christian studies. The following list suggests some of the additional available sources.

ALTHOUSE, LAVONNE. *When Jew and Christian Meet.* New York: Friendship Press, 1966.

BAECK, LEO. *The Essence of Judaism.* New York: Schocken Books, 1961.

———. *Judaism and Christianity.* Philadelphia: Jewish Publication Society of America, 1958.

———. *This People Israel: The Meaning of Jewish Existence.* New York: Holt, Rinehart and Winston, 1965.

BARTH, MARKUS. *Israel and the Church. Contribution to a Dialogue Vital for Peace.* Richmond: John Knox Press, 1969.

BOROWITZ, EUGENE. *New Jewish Theology in the Making.* Philadelphia: Westminster Press, 1968.

BOVIER, RICHARD, *et al. The Study of Judaism: Bibliographical Essays.* New York: Ktav Publishing House, Inc., 1972.

BUBER, MARTIN. *The Prophetic Faith.* New York: Harper & Row, 1960.

———. *Two Types of Faith: The Interpenetration of Judaism and Christianity.* New York: Harper & Row, 1961.

DAVIES, ALAN T. *Antisemitism and the Christian Mind: The Crisis of Conscience after Auschwitz.* New York: Herder & Herder, 1969.

Dialog. Vol. 6: "The Jews" (Summer 1967).

ECKARDT, ALICE AND A. ROY. *Encounter with Israel: A Challenge to Conscience.* New York: Association Press, 1970.

FRIEDLANDER, ALBERT H., ed. *Out of the Whirlwind: A Reader on Holocaust Literature.* New York: Doubleday, 1968.

GORDIS, ROBERT. *The Root and the Branch: Judaism and the Free Society.* Chicago: University of Chicago Press, 1962.

HALPERN, BEN. *The Idea of the Jewish State.* Cambridge: Harvard University Press, 1967.

HESCHEL, ABRAHAM J. *The Prophets.* New York: Harper & Row, 1962.

ISAAC, JULES. *Jesus and Israel.* New York: Holt, Rinehart and Winston, 1971.

———. *The Teaching of Contempt: Christian Roots of Anti-Semitism.* New York: Holt, Rinehart and Winston, 1964.

KATZ, JACOB. *Exclusiveness and Tolerance: Studies in Jewish-Gentile Relations in Medieval and Modern Times.* New York: Schocken Books, 1962.

KELLEY, DEAN AND OLSON, BERNHARD E. *The Meaning and Conduct of Dialogue.* New York: National Conference of Christians and Jews, n.d.

Lutheran Quarterly. Vol. 20: "Tensions in Jewish-Christian Relations" (August 1968).

Lutheran World. Vol. 10: "The Church and the Jews" (October 1963).

Lutheran World. Vol. 11: "Christians, Jews and the Mission of the Church" (July 1964).

OLSON, BERNHARD E. *Faith and Prejudice: Intergroup Problems in Protestant Curricula.* New Haven: Yale University Press, 1963.

———. *Homework for Christians Preparing for Jewish-Christian Dialogue.* New York: National Conference of Christians and Jews, n.d.

PARKES, JAMES W. *Whose Land: A History of the Peoples of Palestine.* New York: Taplinger, 1971.

———. *Antisemitism.* Chicago: Quadrangle Books, 1969.

———. *Prelude to Dialogue: Jewish-Christian Relationships.* New York: Schocken Books, 1969.

ROTH, LEON. *Judaism, A Portrait.* New York: Schocken Books, 1972.

SANDMEL, SAMUEL. *We Jews and Jesus.* Fair Lawn, N.J.: Oxford University Press, 1965.

———. *We Jews and You Christians.* Philadelphia: Lippincott, 1967.

STENDAHL, KRISTER. "Judaism and Christianity: Then and Now," in *New Theology*, No. 2. Martin E. Marty and Dean G. Peerman, eds. New York: The Macmillan Company, 1965, pp. 153–164.